WHAT IS THE CHURCH?

WHAT IS
the Church?

A Symposium of Baptist Thought

Compiled and Edited by
Duke K. McCall

BROADMAN PRESS

Nashville, Tennessee

Library of Congress catalog card number: 58-5411

Printed in the United States of America

5. JUL 57 KSP

PREFACE

For two successive summers a group of Baptist ministers gathered on the campus of the Southern Baptist Theological Seminary to study the doctrine of the church. Most of them were Southern Baptists, but this was more the result of the acquaintanceship of the committee which issued the invitations than of any deliberate plan. The second of the two meetings was held at the same time as a session of the Executive Committee of the Baptist World Alliance. Thus it was possible for some Baptists from overseas, including some members of a Baptist World Alliance Commission on the Doctrine of the Church, to participate in the discussion.

The chapters of this book are some of the papers read. In an atmosphere of genuine Christian fellowship each paper was discussed at length. There was never a sense of having plumbed any subject completely, and indeed there were sharp edges of disagreement about what was said at some points.

When it was proposed that these papers be issued in printed form, there were two completely opposite reactions. On the one hand there was delight at the prospect of sharing and testing the ideas and information with a larger group. On the other hand there were grave misgivings as to whether compressed discussions written for the minds of friendly critics would not be misunderstood or even, if understood, create unchristian controversy. There was unanimity at only one point, namely, that Baptists need to take their bearings on the important doctrine of the church. Within the Southern Baptist

Convention more than half a century has passed since the last serious, general discussion of the church. Unfortunately that discussion became so involved in personalities that sight of the real issues was lost. May that not happen again.

But that there will be discussion of the popular ideas about the church in the light of new information herein contained or old information brought again to attention is eagerly anticipated. To expect that this discussion will end in a unanimous verdict is perhaps optimistic. Baptists, however, who have no ecclesiastical court or infallible ecclesiastic, must be able to test the truth of any proposition in the arena of free discussion where final authority is always the revelation of God.

The author of each paper has stated his own position. The editor has attempted only to adapt papers, prepared to be read to others who had done considerable study in the doctrine of the church, for the general reader. While it is obvious that there is much agreement among the authors, particularly with reference to certain historical facts, each one would have written the others' chapters in a different way.

Since the original papers were prepared for Baptists, many obvious points on which Baptists are in general agreement are ignored. This does not mean that they are unimportant. For example, only casual reference is made to immersion as the mode of baptism or to the fact that the predominant number of references to the church in the New Testament refer to a gathered congregation in a specific place. Essentially this volume is not concerned with ground already won but rather with matters where ideas and understanding are still being tested in the warfare of opinions.

It is hoped that the reader will accept this composite study of the church as an invitation to investigation and thought on the subject himself.

DUKE K. McCALL

CONTENTS

Preface
DUKE K. McCALL v

Introduction
W. O. CARVER 1

I. The Nature of the Church
DALE MOODY 15

II. The Origin of the Church
R. W. KICKLIGHTER 28

III. The Ministry in the New Testament Churches
S. A. NEWMAN 46

IV. The Doctrine of Baptism in the New Testament
T. C. SMITH 62

V. The New Testament Significance of the Lord's
Supper
DALE MOODY 79

vii

VI. The Anabaptist View of the Church
   THERON D. PRICE 97

VII. The Beginnings of Baptist Churches
   ROBERT G. TORBET 118

VIII. The Landmark Movement in the Southern Baptist
   Convention
   JOHN E. STEELY 134

IX. An Interpretation of Christian Stewardship
   PAUL L. STAGG 148

X. Discipline in the Church
   THERON D. PRICE 164

About the Writers   186

INTRODUCTION

W. O. Carver

THE NATURE OF THE CHURCH is at the very center of urgent
theological considerations at present. Its importance grows
out of several aspects of world conditions and of their impact on, and challenge to, organized Christianity.

First of all is the fact of the unfinished task of the Christian
gospel. This is pressed in on the consciousness of alert Christians by the surging tides of materialism and of revolution
which are more universal and more radical than ever before
in history. Any who are not blind to the confused assertive-
ness of peoples throughout the world are forced to recognize
this fact. After eighteen centuries of gospel expansion, humanity is still largely unevangelized and still pagan in its pattern of living. One cannot escape the question of whether
the churches have properly envisioned and seriously assumed
the responsibilities of their meaning and message in the mind
of the redeeming Christ.

As Christians face the questions that arise, they see how
relatively ineffective their influence on the life of the world is.
There is need for all to recognize the weakness of the present
Christian movement in organization, concepts, and methods
for giving a full Christian witness in "this present evil age."

At the same time, no man who shares in any adequate measure the passion of Christ can overlook the need of the world
in every way for the witness of the Christian gospel.

1

The demand for unity of spirit and aim within organized Christianity, and the ever-increasing demands for institutional and organizational union of Protestantism make the matter of the true nature of the church of Jesus Christ a matter of primary concern to all who take their Christianity seriously. Within the last sixty years interest in the subject of "divided Christendom" has been growing gradually until "the ecumenical movement" now holds the center of attention for many Christian leaders.

The urgent efforts of evangelical leadership in the last quarter century to organize institutional Christianity around some common center have brought awareness of the key importance of "the church." But while this is true, discussions have made clear that there is confusion as to the nature of the church. The connotation of the term is obscure among those who are eager to work toward unification of the evangelical witness of this age.

The New Testament Foundation

By no means is there general agreement among leaders of various denominations that the New Testament provides an authoritative norm for the nature and functions of the church, but it is coming to be recognized that there is no other starting point for exploring the possibilities of union or even of unity. All Christians bring to New Testament study conceptions and misconceptions which have developed in the course of their varied and divergent denominational histories. Specific forms, traditions, and dogmatic formulas have not only become dear but also have conditioned thinking until they may be regarded as absolute truths.

An objective, inductive study of the New Testament will yield no explicit, detailed description of the church. Basic principles underlie all the New Testament writings; for details and uniformity, students seek in vain. The apostles and prophets and pastors and teachers in the New Testament era did not think in the terms of twentieth-century problems about the church. Many today demand detailed authority, but the inspired writers seem to have lacked any sense of this need. Apart from embryonic movements, the New Testament leaders knew no denominational-type divisions. Tendencies in that direction were opposed with great earnestness, dealt with in the spirit of love and fellowship, and checked short of any actual division throughout the apostolic period.

Since the New Testament nowhere has an explicit definition or description of the church, basic and determinative criteria must be reached by inductive study of the New Testament books. Dogmatic affirmations based on modern ideas and forms cannot be accepted as determinative. They are the result of developments in the course of history under influences narrowing the significance of Christ's incarnation and the divine nature of the true Christian movement. Multiple lines of historical development have given rise to the conflicting ecclesiological theories and ecclesiastical forms of present-day organized Christianity.

The teachings of Jesus in the Gospels contain nothing explicit about the church. Only one of the four evangelists recalled that Jesus used the term "church," and he recorded its use on only two occasions. In the first of these (Matt. 16), the concept is wholly spiritual and its origin attributed definitely to divine revelation. The second instance (Matt. 18) implies, without any explanation, a brotherhood having social and organizational aspects. There also is implied very definitely a supersocial, divinely induced quality. Without using the term "church" or offering a definition of any equivalent, the other Gospels assume the spiritual reality that constitutes the church.

Acts, "the Gospel of the Holy Spirit," is the first chapter in the history of the expansion of the gospel and the Christian movement under the guidance and by the power of the Spirit. Again no attention is devoted to the nature of the church as such. Rather, there are simple records of facts, acts, and incidental information as to organization, leaders (never officials), and functional activities of the apostles, prophets, evangelists, and the experiences and witness of other believers.

In the Epistles the churches have organizations, and the forms of their organizations are taken for granted. They are never defined or described in any detail. Bishops and deacons as such are recognized only in Philippians and the pastoral epistles. It is going quite beyond recorded facts to find anything approaching the idea of "orders of the ministry" in any part of the New Testament. "Elders" are named in Acts 11 as recipients of the relief funds brought from Antioch. There is no previous mention of them and no description of their function.

Deacons had been chosen earlier, and their qualities and qualifications are described in Acts 6. Even there they are not so named, but the name is implied in the use of the verb. Their duties arose out of an emergency situation. There is no indication that they were considered officers or that their role was continued after the emergency. The function of these, enlarged under a later emergency, was vested in the "elders" mentioned in chapter 11. In both cases, and as a principle in all similar cases, these were not officials. Rather, they were servants of the brotherhood. There are lists of offices and functions within the brotherhood in Romans 12, 1 Corinthians 12, and Ephesians 4. These differ widely, and the study of the differences leads to two conclusions: first, that there was no standard form, imposed or recognized, for the details of church organization; second, that there was no emphasis on official status or standing. The emphasis is in every case on service in the interest of the unity, the harmony, and the effectiveness of the church as the witness of the redeeming gospel.

All four classes of leadership mentioned in Ephesians are "gifts" of the risen, ascended, and administering Christ in order to develop a devoted, redeemed humanity. The functions of these four groups all tend primarily to the extension and the establishment of Christian centers in various geographical divisions. The first three have to do with bringing the gospel to new regions and helping those who receive it to begin Christian living. The work of "apostles, prophets, evangelists" prepares for, and culminates in, the work of "pastors and teachers" (two functions of the same group). These latter lead in the developing of the converts in their duties, their function, their organization, their Christian living "worthy of the gospel." Paul said that the function of each group looks to the equipment of all the saints for the work of ministering. The ultimate end is a continuous, harmonious, effective progress of the entire body, ever increasing in love as it becomes the "body of the Christ."

Although it provides no definition or detailed description of the church, the New Testament does use various terms which, by direct implication and by rich and varied symbolism, provide materials for understanding the nature of the church, universal and local. Most of the information available, of course, deals with details of the function and of the conduct of churches as local organizations. These are "the churches of God," as in Corinthians and Revelation. They are the "churches of Christ" and often simply "the church" or "the churches." While never called churches of the Holy Spirit, their relation to the Spirit is abundantly implied and declared. He works in them and through them as the power of God, the interpreter of Christ, the guide, the purifier, and developer of the church bodies.

The universal church and its local manifestations as congregations are distinctly divine in origin and in meaning. They are God's creation, the people of God, and of his Christ. They constitute a new humanity produced, preserved, and empowered as God's representative in the midst of "all the families of the earth." The church is the congregation of the true Israel of God, continuing, interpreting, and supplanting the Old Testament Israel in terms of "God's saints in Christ Jesus."

The description of Israel in the plan of God in Exodus 19:4–6 is appropriated almost word for word in 1 Peter 2:8–10 as the description of the body of Christian believers. In the Old Testament God's people are frequently called "God's heritage," and Paul used the same term for the Christian church in Ephesians. Recent emphasis is sound in recognizing the historical and spiritual unity of the people of God in the Old Testament and in the New Testament. Yet it is not always clearly seen that Jesus at the close of his ministry (Matt. 21–22), with two powerful parables to illustrate his point, explicitly repudiated Israel—as understood by Jewish leaders of his day. Jewish people as such were no longer to be the husbandmen of God's vineyard. This new Israel was the new creation of God in Christ Jesus. It was to be the church of God in Christ Jesus.

This "new humanity" consists of those who have accepted God's grace and have committed themselves to it. Because of their dedication, they are designated throughout the New Testament by the term "saints." These sanctified individuals voluntarily unite—as a church in the local sense—to give expression to their common experience of redemption, through worship, fellowship, and witnessing to the gospel of the Lord Jesus Christ.

Fellowship or brotherhood is the outstanding characteristic of New Testament Christians and of all Christians of succeeding ages to the degree that they are truly Christian.

Each group of believers becomes in its own location the body of Christ. Each is "distinctly a temple of God in the Holy Spirit" and is so sacred that whoever destroys it will himself be destroyed (1 Cor. 3:17). Its unity, its fellowship, its representative character is such that factions and divisions in that body divide Christ and bring his condemnation (1 Cor. 10:14). Each member of each church is "baptized into the fellowship" and repudiates or neglects that fellowship to his own sickness and even spiritual death. Paul emphasized this by teaching that participation in the Lord's Supper is "fellowship in the body of Christ," whose unity is symbolized and enforced by the one loaf and the one cup.

The congregation, a local manifestation of the church, begins in, and follows from, the fact that the total body of the redeemed constitutes the continuing, growing body of Christ. While the exact expression is never used, this comprehensive spiritual church is the continuation of the incarnation. In the book of Ephesians Christ and the church are so intimately related as to constitute one entity, neither being complete except in relation to the other. It is "in the church and in Christ Jesus" that God is to be glorified throughout all generations of the age of the ages. By the fact of his salvation the believer becomes a member of the church, "a member of the body of Christ." Under the impulse of the Spirit, this member of the spiritual church voluntarily takes his place in the local fellowship and assumes his responsibility as a Christian in that church, for that local church is a concrete, organized expression of the one spiritual church. This conception of the one church as the body of the Christ is more than a figure of speech. It is a spiritual reality apart from which there is no salvation and no true Christianity.

This total fellowship of the saints, this new humanity, is God's "household," his "family," his "commonwealth," of which all believers are alike members, whatever their social or religious background. All of these children of God created in Christ Jesus constitute the temple of God in the earth for his indwelling (Eph. 2). In the measure of its genuineness and integration and unity and love and its loyalty to its Head, each congregation is, in its situation, God's local humanity, Christ's local body, God's temple. Each local congregation is for its community "the pillar and ground of the truth." It is an association of evangelistic witnesses; it is the guardian of the "true gospel."

The unity and glory of the spiritual church as the body of Christ is emphasized in Ephesians 5, where the relation between Christ and his church is set out as the ideal for that between husband and wife. In view of the biblical figure of the church as Christ's bride, the insistence of some that all uses of the term "church" in the New Testament refer only to local organizations becomes absurd almost to the point of sacrilege, attributing to Christ a bride in every locality where a church is found. Likewise the term "body of Christ" in Ephesians 1 and 2 cannot be restricted to local organized bodies. How can one conceive of any one local church as being "the full expression of him who is fulfilling all things in all respects"? How can one conceive of independent local bodies as growing into "one holy temple of God in the Holy Spirit," especially when the whole context of the paragraph emphasizes the unity of all members of the new human race produced by the cross of Christ? How can the concept of the church in the development of chapter 3 be limited to the independent local body which is to attain "unto all the fulness of God"? How can this limited group be the medium of God's glory forever "in the church and in Christ Jesus"? How can the "one body" as presented in the transcendent concepts of Ephesians 4:1-16 be restricted at any point to a local church?

Historic Misinterpretations

The church as it has developed through history and as it stands "in the present divided state of Christendom" has experienced radical misinterpretations, and these misinterpretations now dominate the scene and hinder progress toward "the unity of the Spirit in the bond of peace," which more and more clamors for recognition and expression.

The first and most persistent and damaging is the theory of treating the church as an institution. Some of the more radical evils of this misconception I have discussed in my book *The Glory of God in the Christian Calling*. Emil Brunner has, in his recent work *The Misunderstanding of the Church*, radically exposed this same error. He shows how this mistaken conception works as the inciting factor in the search for unity and especially in all schemes for ecclesiastical union.

Akin to this is the view of the church as primarily an organization. Never in the New Testament is the matter of organization primary, never is it stressed nor even clearly defined in any instance. There are certain dominant principles and ideas which must be preserved if the integrity of the gospel is preserved. Yet these principles and ideas do not find uniform expression in any detailed pattern of organization.

In addition to these misinterpretations of the church as such, certain mistaken emphases within historic Christianity have diverted and corrupted the church. The first of these is authoritative creed. All creeds and all confessions of faith are formulated and adopted in a contemporary context. They well serve their purposes of defining experience and conviction provided they are not taken as timeless, authoritative norms for creating experience and controlling new experience and Christian duty under all conditions and circumstances.

Emphasis on ritual likewise has curbed freedom of spirit and expression in worship and tends to become a hindrance to the Holy Spirit in his direct redemptive activity in individual lives. Creed and ritual too often contribute to lifting the worshipers beyond the obligations, constraints, and restraints of ethical Christianity, and of creative thinking. Ritualism is the great enemy to vital Christianity.

At the heart of the evils of ritual is the concept of the "sacrament." In itself the sacramental conception of the usefulness of material symbols for spiritual meditation and for the development of spiritual insight is not bad—and may be very helpful. This is especially true of the two symbols, baptism and the Lord's Supper, which were practiced in the early churches and which come directly from the teachings of Jesus. However, the tendency to attach magical significance to physical objects results in an interpretation of the "sacraments" that is deceitful, corrupting, and destructive of genuine experience of God.

There also are misconceptions about membership in the Christian church and in the churches. The different views and the variant practices in this matter attest the inherent evils of the departure from the basic individualism of Christian experience and responsibility, without which there can be no vital Christians nor genuine Christianity.

Finally there are misconceptions about the relation of the church and churches to the "kingdom of God" and also to "the people of the convenant of Israel." These latter concepts are distinct from each other, and both have largely been either overlooked or vaguely dealt with by many Christian leaders. They have become items of much study and concern by leaders of the ecumenical movement. Especially are these leaders disturbed and confused over practical questions of fellowship in the Eucharist; and about the relationship of Israel in the Old Testament to the church of the New Testament.

Present Implications

The holy people of God, the Old Testament Israel, reconstituted but continued in the New Testament, are a special creation of God in the midst of, and out of, the human material found in empirical world history. They are an elect race in the body of humanity. In a unique sense the church is the creation and the continuation of the redeeming Christ, Son of the living God. On the rock of this regenerating experience and its relation of men to God in himself as its foundation, Jesus said, "I will build my congregation."

Just as the seed of Abraham were claimed by God from among all the sons of men, the remnant was chosen out of the generally unfaithful people of Israel to be God's heritage. When Christ came to press his claim to his people and his kingdom, he found the descendants of the remnant unfit and unwilling to be his people. Thus he rejected the old remnant and lifted the calling of God above the racial and institutional understanding of the Jews by showing its true meaning, a renewal experience in which man and God are united in Christ. This union of God and believing man, with all its consequences, has for its basic principle "faith working through love." To the old remnant, which had failed to accept and fulfil the purpose of God in history, Jesus declared, "The kingdom of God will be taken away from you and given to a nation producing the fruits of it" (Matt. 21:43, RSV). The new people who would become Christ's "elect race" were the people of his choice, a dedicated people who would exhibit Christ's own excellencies. It was to this new spiritual reality that Christ referred when he spoke of "my church." Here is the primary base for all understanding of the one Christian church and of the local churches in which the one church realizes itself in objective experience and manifestation.

Our Baptist forebears had the right approach in defining the church. They began with the spiritually regenerate church and proceeded to define its individual "societies" as its functional agencies. See, for example, the London Confession of 1689 and its American counterpart, the Philadelphia Confession.

No church in the New Testament is an institution. Nor is any church in the New Testament ever primarily or essentially an organization. The organizations are functional expressions of the underlying reality. Certain kinds of activities grow out of the church's nature and are required for effectiveness under any conditions. Various other activities are required under special conditions: hence the variety in the lists of offices, duties, and gifts in Romans 12:3–8; 1 Corinthians 12:27–30; and Ephesians 4:11. Only in Philippians 1 and 1 Timothy 3 are the two officer groups, bishops and deacons, so named. In light of the whole New Testament it cannot be asserted that these two classes of leaders are thought of as officials in the church or even as essential to the reality of a church.

Any true church is primarily a creation of the Spirit of God. God's redemptive act is its starting point, followed by each man's response to God's work. After these events comes the corporate human-divine fellowship. Each church thus has three aspects: God, the redeemed individual, and the fellowship. And in all these aspects each church should be consciously related to the whole body of Christ, through which God is functioning in redemption.

The church, therefore, is God's "new creation," a new humanity in the midst of unredeemed humanity; a local church is a concrete embodiment of this church.

The church is the extension of the incarnation. A local church is the manifestation of Christ in its community.

The church is the body of Christ, who is himself the fulness of God in redemption; a local church is the functioning of the redeemed body in a fellowship of redeemed men.

The church is the core of God's kingdom as being realized in human history. Local churches are the agencies of that kingdom and of its gospel; thus they are "colonies" of the kingdom of heaven on earth, located in the midst of the world which is to be won through the gospel. They are not only emigration centers for heaven but are also recruiting agencies and training instruments and supervising bodies for the recruits as they become active workers in the gospel.

The wide differences of denominations in organized Christianity—the misplaced emphases which each, in some way, embodies—confront everyone who is conscious of his membership in the body of the Christ with incompatible challenges to loyalty. No one can give unquestioning loyalty to his own denomination and at the same time devote himself fully to the fellowship of the spiritual church. Denominations have within themselves distinctive divisions which cultivate special loyalties. We Baptists are far from recognizing that thoroughgoing loyalty to Christ ought to sanctify and give deeper meaning to our loyalties to our denominational organizations. All Christians are apt to justify their separateness and even isolationism on the ground that they have to be loyal to the truth, claiming that, after all, it is the truth that divides.

Christians are faced constantly with a dilemma. Is it possible for them to be loyal to the truth in the deepest sense without being even more fundamentally loyal to the purpose, the passion, and the person of him who is the Saviour of their souls and the Lord of their lives, the Head of every group that names his name as a church of Jesus Christ? Either there is a living tension or else contentment with lesser loyalty is achieved by some narrowing dogmatism that repudiates full loyalty to Christ as Head of the entire spiritual body.

Here is a problem for all organizations within the Christian movement, one which demands rethinking in the larger light of God's purpose for the world. No local church and no denomination can come into the fulness of Christ's fellowship and experience without relating itself in its thoughts, its prayers, and its plans to all the saints who see the kingdom of God as the realm into which men are brought through the second birth by the working of the Holy Spirit. If any denomination or church shall say, "I am not of the body," is it, therefore, not of the body? If it shall say of any other church or denomination, "You are not of the body," is that other group, therefore, not of the body? If any denomination shall say, "We are alone the body," is that denomination the entire body? Must we not all come to grips with these questions, seeking the guidance of the Word and Spirit of God to strengthen the very imperfect expression the "Christian" world is giving to the meaning and mission of Christ Jesus?

The church in the New Testament never appears as an organized body, nor do the churches ever combine in territorial organizations. From that basic fact Baptists proceed in accepting and developing their call to membership in the spiritual fellowship with all who are in Christ.

I

THE NATURE OF THE CHURCH

Dale Moody

THE NATURE OF THE CHURCH in the New Testament has been obscured by the historical misunderstandings of ecclesiastical conflict. Augustine's distinction between the earthly city (*civitas terrena*) and the heavenly city (*civitas Dei*) has been perverted in Roman Catholicism by the identification of the historical institution with the heavenly ideal; yet for Augustine the church, while participating in the *civitas Dei*, is not identical with the ideal until the end of history. Likewise the state, while participating in the *civitas terrena*, is not identical with earthly evil; to become identical would mean its own destruction.[1] Calvin's distinction between the visible and the invisible church is strikingly similar to Augustine's distinction between the ideal and the institutional.[2]

This distinction in Augustine and Calvin was a tenet of the Particular Baptists in England. The Baptist Confession of the seven London congregations in 1644, the first Baptist confession of the Calvinistic type, says:

XLVII. And although the particular Congregations be distinct and severall Bodies, every one a compact and knit Citie in it selfe; yet are they all to walk by one and the same Rule, and by all means convenient to have the counsell and help one of

[1] Ernest Barker, "Introduction," *The City of God*, trans. John Healey (New York: E. P. Dutton and Co., 1931), pp. xvi–xxxii.

[2] John Calvin, *Institutes of the Christian Religion*, trans. John Allen (Grand Rapids: Wm. B. Eerdman's Publishing Company, 1949), II, 269–273.

another in all needfull affaires of *the Church, as members of one body in the common faith under Christ their onely head.* [3]

After the historic Westminster Confession, generally accepted as the classic exposition of Calvinism, was presented to Parliament in 1646, almost all Particular Baptist confessions followed it except in regard to believer's baptism and congregational government. The Particular Baptist Confession of 1677, reaffirmed in 1689, was "adopted by the Baptist Association met at Philadelphia, September 25, 1742," and by both the Charleston Association in South Carolina and the Warren Association in Rhode Island in 1767. It represents classic Baptist Calvinism. The nature of the church is described as follows:

The Catholick or universal Church, which (with respect to internal work of the Spirit, and truth of grace) may be called invisible, consists of the whole number of the Elect, that have been, are, or shall be gathered into one, under Christ the head thereof; and is the spouse, the body, the fulness of him that filleth all in all. [4]

The Charleston Summary of Church Discipline, a document filled with amazing insight, said the church when "considered collectively forms one complete and glorious body" and "is the general assembly and church of the first born." [5]

The priority of the spiritual organism over the institutional organization is obvious in all this great theological stream. It is clearly summarized in the Abstract of Principles adopted by the Southern Baptist Theological Seminary, April 30, 1858. Article XIV of that historic document reads:

[3] W. J. McGlothlin, *Baptist Confessions of Faith* (Philadelphia: American Baptist Publication Society, 1911), pp. 186 f.; italics added.
[4] *Ibid.*, p. 264.
[5] Chapter I, p. 3 (from the 1850 printing by B. Temple at Raleigh, N. C., bound with the Charleston Confession and a catechism).

The Lord Jesus is the Head of the Church, which is composed of all his true disciples, and in Him is invested supremely all power for its government. According to his commandment, Christians are to associate themselves into particular societies or Churches; and to each of these Churches he hath given needful authority for administering that order, discipline and worship which he hath appointed. The regular officers of a Church are Bishops or Elders, and Deacons.

It is, therefore, no surprise to read a long and lucid chapter on "The Church Universal" as well as one on "Local Churches" in the first textbook in systematic theology used in the Southern Baptist Theological Seminary.[6] Many Southern Baptists, unaware of the facts of Southern Baptist history and unmoved by the plain teachings of the New Testament, have followed the innovations of Landmarkism which infiltrated into the South from the North through such personalities as J. R. Graves and J. M. Pendleton.[7]

Even the preface of the New Hampshire Confession of Faith in 1833 expresses the hope that it would "be blessed by the great Head of the Church to promote still more that delightful harmony of sentiment and ardent brotherly love which now exists in so eminent a degree among our churches." [8] Article XIII defines "a visible Church of Christ" and is therefore not in conflict with the use of "the Church" in the preface.

To use P. T. Forsyth's metaphor, the local congregation is the "outcrop" of the church composed of all true believers.

[6] J. L. Dagg, "A Treatise on Church Order," *Manual of Theology*, Second Part (Charleston: Southern Baptist Publication Society, 1859), pp. 74–143.

[7] W. W. Barnes, *The Southern Baptist Convention* (Nashville: Broadman Press, 1954), pp. 100–117.

[8] *New Hampshire Baptist Register*, January 20, 1833. Quoted from Charles Riley MacDonald, "New Hampshire Declaration of Faith" (unpublished doctoral dissertation in Northern Baptist Theological Seminary, Chicago, May, 1939), pp. 52 f.

As the "outcrop" is of the same nature as the formation of which it is a part, so the local congregation shares the nature of the body of Christ.[9] Rigid distinction between the local assembly and the general assembly, especially when the general assembly as the body of Christ is rejected, is a case of not being able to see the woods for the trees. The spiritual nature of the local assembly is so identical with the general assembly that it is impossible to have a local church if it is not composed of regenerate members of the body of Christ. Local societies not composed of such regenerate members are, in the words of the Particular Baptist Confession of 1677, "Synagogues of Satan." The church is that fellowship of faith created by the living God as Father, Son, and Holy Spirit to the praise of his glory. Apart from God no other agency, in heaven or on earth, is adequate to create, continue, or complete this spiritual organism. "Membership in the church universal," declared the saintly J. L. Dagg, "is determined by God himself." [10]

The Church in Relation to God

The question of the relationship between the church and God is raised by the use of the terms "the church of God" (1 Cor. 1:2; 10:32; 11:32; 15:9; 2 Cor. 1:1; Gal. 1:13; 1 Tim. 3:5, 15) and "the churches of God" (1 Thess. 2:14; 1 Cor. 11:16) in the New Testament.

First, the church is presented as *the people of God*. A passage such as 1 Peter 1:3 to 2:10 relates the concept of the church to the people of God in the Old Testament. Against the background of the work of the Father (1:3–6), the Son (1:7–9), and the Holy Spirit (1:10–12), God's redemption

[9] Cf. Ernest A. Payne, *The Fellowship of Believers* (London: The Carey Kingsgate Press, 1954), p. 29, n. 6.
[10] J. L. Dagg, *op. cit.*, p. 143.

of his people is described in the figures of an exodus (1:13–21), a life (1:22 to 2:3), and a house (2:4–10). The description of the new exodus made possible by "the precious blood of Christ" (1:19) is filled with allusions to the Old Testament Exodus. The new life, also explained in Old Testament language, is produced by spiritual seed (1:22–25) and nurtured by spiritual milk (2:1–2). And, finally, the new house is described with a constellation of Old Testament quotations (2:4–8). Writing "to the exiles of the dispersion in Pontus, Galatia, Cappadocia, Asia, and Bithynia, chosen and destined by God the Father and sanctified by the Spirit for obedience to Jesus Christ and for sprinkling with his blood," Peter can say:

But you are a chosen race, a royal priesthood, a holy nation, God's own people, that you may declare the wonderful deeds of him who called you out of darkness into his marvelous light. Once you were no people but now you are God's people; once you had not received mercy but now you have received mercy. (1 Pet. 2:9–10, RSV)

Second, the Church is presented as *the temple of God*. This figure, evident in 1 Peter 2:4–10, is elaborated by Paul and John. In 2 Corinthians 6:14 to 7:1 the whole point of the appeal, containing five rhetorical questions and three quotations from the Old Testament, which calls for separation from pagan immorality, is summed up in the statement that "we are the temple of the living God" (6:16, RSV). First Corinthians 3:10–17 expands this "temple" terminology by declaring Jesus Christ the foundation upon which may be built "gold, silver, precious stones, wood, hay, stubble" to be tested by fire in the day of judgment (3:10–15). The frightful thing about spiritual sacrilege, that is, schism in the church, is found in the fact that God will destroy those who destroy his temple. And this temple is composed of those in whom God's Spirit dwells (3:16 f.).

A third passage in Paul, Ephesians 2:11–22, brings the temple concept to a climax. Those alienated from God (2:11 f.) have been reconciled to God through the blood of the cross of Christ (2:13–16). Christ, who is our peace (2:14) and who makes peace (2:15), preaches peace to those far off and to those who are near (2:17) by breaking down the dividing wall of human hostility (2:14) in the temple of God. The result of reconciliation follows (2:19–22, RSV):

So then you are no longer strangers and sojourners, but you are fellow citizens with the saints and members of the household of God, built upon the foundation of the apostles and prophets, Christ Jesus himself being the chief cornerstone, in whom the whole structure is joined together and grows into a holy temple in the Lord; in whom you also are built into it for a dwelling place of God in the Spirit.

It is highly probable that the Gospel of John, written to persuade the readers "that Jesus is the Christ, the Son of God" (20:31), intends for the reader to see Jesus as the new temple taking the place of the Temple in Jerusalem that is destroyed. The cleansing of the Temple at the first of three Passover feasts (2:13) is not without theological significance. The discussion about the destruction of the Temple in contrast to the death of Jesus is not left ambiguous. Plainly it is said: "But he spoke of the temple of his body. When therefore he was raised from the dead, his disciples remembered that he had said this; and they believed the scripture and the word which Jesus had spoken" (John 2:21–22, RSV).

The Church in Relation to Jesus Christ

It has been impossible to speak of *the people of God* and *the temple of God* apart from Jesus Christ and the Holy

Spirit, but a clearer understanding of the relationship between Jesus Christ and the church appears in Paul's use of the metaphors of *the body of Christ* and *the bride of Christ*. Indeed, it is not beyond probability that the Gospel of John implies these two relations by the emphasis given the miracle of turning water into wine at the marriage of Cana and the prediction about the temple of Jesus' body in the cleansing of the Temple. However that may be, there is no mistake about these metaphors in Paul.

The church as the *body of Christ* can best be understood against the Hebrew idea of corporate personality, such as is found in the teachings on the Servant of the Lord (Isa. 53), the Son of man (Dan. 7:13–22), and Adam (Rom. 5:12–21). The points of most importance to Paul are the members; then the head, and finally the unity of the body with Jesus Christ as the head.

The members of the body come in for special consideration in a number of passages. In 1 Corinthians 6:15 f. Paul rebukes immorality among Christians on the basis that the bodies of Christians are "members of Christ" as well as the temple of the Holy Spirit. The fact that Christians constitute one body of which all are members is both the basis for saying the loaf at the Lord's Supper is a participation (*koinōnia*) in the body of Christ and the reason for Christians to separate themselves from pagan sacrifices (1 Cor. 10:14–22). Those who participate in the Lord's Supper are warned to examine themselves that they may not bring the judgment of God upon themselves by failing to discern the body of Christ (1 Cor. 11:28 f.). These close associations between the one loaf which represents the body of Christ and the members who constitute the body of Christ have led A. E. J. Rawlinson and a number of other New Testament theologians to conclude that Paul's idea of the body of Christ is derived from the

loaf at the Lord's Supper.[11] Unity in diversity in the church
is based on the belief that "just as the body is one and has
many members, and all the members of the body, though
many, are one body," this unity may be realized by taking
thought that "the body does not consist of one member but
of many" (1 Cor. 12:12, 14, RSV). Those who "have died
to the law through the body of Christ" not only "belong
to another" (Rom. 7:4) but "are one body in Christ, and
individually members one of another" in the functions of
sober Christian living (Rom. 12:5 f.). The body of Christ
is nothing less than the presence of Christ himself in the life
and service of the Christian community.[12] This does not mean
that the church is Christ, but it does mean that there can be
no true church apart from vital union of the members with
Christ.

The head of the body is Christ. In Colossians the idea of
the church as the body of Christ is continued as Paul rejoiced
in the sufferings which "complete what is lacking in Christ's
afflictions for the sake of his body, that is, the church" (Col.
1:24). He exhorted the believers to put on love and let the
peace of Christ to which they "are called in one body"
rule in their hearts (Col. 3:15). In Paul's thought Christ as
the head is used in three ways.[13] First, Christ is the head of
every man, even as the husband is the head of the woman
and God is the head of Christ (1 Cor. 11:3). Second, Christ
is the head of all rule and authority (Col. 2:10), having dis-
armed the principalities and powers by the triumph of the
cross (Col. 2:15) and put them under his feet (Eph. 1:22).

[11] J. Robert Nelson, *The Realm of Redemption* (London: The Epworth
Press, 1951), p. 71.

[12] Eduard Schweitzer, *Das Leben des Herrn in der Gemeinde und ihren
Diensten* (Zurich: Swingli-Verlag, 1946), p. 51.

[13] Elias Andrews, *The Meaning of Christ for Paul* (New York: Abing-
don-Cokesbury Press, 1949), pp. 112–15.

Third, Christ is the head of the church as his body (Col. 1:18). Those who worship angels are "not holding fast to the Head, from whom the whole body, nourished and knit together through its joints and ligaments, grows with a growth that is from God" (Col. 2:19, RSV).

The unity of the body finds fullest expression in Ephesians. The head of the body, as in Colossians, is seen also in Ephesians (1:22; 4:15; 5:23); but the unity of the body, implicit in other places, becomes very explicit. In Ephesians the headship of Christ is described in reference to the past, present, and future. The great prayer for knowledge in Ephesians 1:15–23 is a petition for spiritual enlightenment (1:15–19a) and spiritual energy (1:19b–23) in the light of the resurrection and exaltation of Christ to the right hand of God. Those who believe that this great reality will be postponed to some future time, as if Christ had a body only at the end of history, greatly err. Christ, here and now, is both sovereign over the church and the one who fills it with his presence, so that it "is his body, the fulness of him who fills all in all" (Eph. 1:23). The past reality of the exaltation of Christ is experienced as a present reality in the life of the body.

The unity of life is grounded in the great sevenfold unity: "one body and one Spirit, just as you were called to the one hope that belongs to your call, one Lord, one faith, one baptism, one God and Father of us all, who is above all and through all and in all" (Eph. 4:4–6, RSV). The growth of this unity is realized by the exercise of the gifts bestowed by the exalted Lord (Eph. 4:7–11) as the members build up the body in love (4:12–16). This body, after the analogy of any body, has a beginning, a growth, and a completion in the future presentation of the body as the bride of Christ.

The church as the *bride of Christ* is an idea rooted in the teachings of the Old Testament prophets who spoke of Israel as the unfaithful wife of *Yahweh* and in poetic passages, such as Psalm 45 and the Song of Songs. Some Old Testament scholars, notably T. J. Meek, see a spiritual marriage in the Song of Songs not far removed from the extreme allegorical teachings of prescientific Old Testament study, and it is not at all sure that the literal love story interpretation is the clue to the meaning of this book.[14] The nuptial theme appears in the teachings both of John the Baptist (John 3:25–29) and Jesus (Mark 2:18–28; Matt. 12:39; 16:4; 22:2; 25:1–13; Luke 14:7–11). Apocalyptic eschatology anticipates "the marriage of the Lamb" when "his Bride has made herself ready" for "the marriage supper of the Lamb" (Rev. 19:7–9), and the bride becomes the wife of the Lamb (Rev. 20:9). But, as with the concept of the body of Christ, the church as the bride of Christ finds fullest expression in Paul.

Three passages of Paul have a strong nuptial element. The first is Galatians 4:21–31 where two women are an allegory of two covenants, one being Hagar the slave, who represents Mount Sinai, and the other being Sarah the free woman who represents the Jerusalem above and is the mother of all who, like Isaac, are "children of promise." This is preceded by Paul's travail for the Galatians (4:19) and is based on the prophetic teaching in Isaiah 54:1. The second passage is 2 Corinthians 11:2–3. For Paul, Christ is the "Second Adam" and it is logical for the church to be compared to Eve. The Corinthian Christians were betrothed to Christ as "a pure bride to her one husband," but there was always the danger that the serpent who deceived Eve would lead the church away from the pure devotion to Christ. The third passage is Ephesians 5:21–23. As in the metaphor of the body, "the husband is the head of the wife as Christ is the head of the church,"

---

[14] Claude Chavasse, *The Bride of Christ* (London: Faber & Faber, Ltd., 1940), pp. 27–45.

and the wife is to be subject to the husband as the church is subject to Christ. Here Paul went beyond the relation of husband and wife so far that he ended by saying he was really talking about "Christ and the church." The husband is to measure his love for his wife by the love Christ had for the church and by the love the husband has for his own body. Paul's thoughts not only flow back and forth between the Christ-church and the husband-wife relation but the metaphors of the body and the bride blend into one. The roots of these relations are found in God's intention for the family and the church, as revealed in Genesis 2:24.

The Church in Relation to the Holy Spirit

The Holy Spirit transforms the sociological phenomenon, subject to the laws of other social groups, into a spiritual fellowship (*koinōnia*) with a ministry (*diakonia*) of service. The fellowship of the Spirit is a term found only twice in the New Testament (2 Cor. 13:14; Phil. 2:1), but the idea supplements the fellowship with the Father (1 John 1:3) and the fellowship with the Son (1 John 1:3; 1 Cor. 1:9) to give the very essence of the church. Devotion "to the apostles' teaching and fellowship, to the breaking of bread and the prayers" (Acts 2:42, RSV) is something more than voluntary association with one another or the participation in the Spirit. It is nothing less than the access through Christ, in the Spirit, to the Father (Eph. 2:18) by all who have been reconciled to God through the blood of the cross of Christ. A thin theology can only lead to a thin ecclesiology.

The fellowship (*koinōnia*) of the Spirit may be summarized with three New Testament terms: the baptism of the Spirit, the gift of the Spirit, and the unity of the Spirit.

The baptism of the Spirit distinguishes the baptism of Jesus from the baptism of John the Baptist (Mark 1:8; Matt.

3:11; Luke 3:16; John 1:33; Acts 1:5; 11:15 f.). The two baptisms are closely associated in Acts, but it is evident in the experience of the Samaritans (Acts 8:14–24), Cornelius (Acts 10:44–48), and the disciples at Ephesus (Acts 19:1–7) that the connection is not so inseparable that one must receive the two together. This close association continues in 1 Corinthians 10:1–4; 12:13. Just as the fathers were baptized into Moses and ate the spiritual food and drank the spiritual drink in the wilderness experience of the old Exodus, so now in the new exodus (1 Cor. 10:11) "by one Spirit we were all baptized into one body—Jews or Greeks, slaves or free— and all were made to drink of one Spirit" (1 Cor. 12:13).

The gift of the Spirit (Luke 11:13; John 3:34; Acts 2:38; 8:20; 10:45; 11:17) is closely associated with baptism. God imparts the Spirit in baptism, as in the laying on of hands and the invoking of the name of Jesus Christ. Any effort, however, to chain the gift of the Spirit to any one of these three acts is refuted by the examples in the book of Acts. Slavery of the Spirit to sacramental rituals is not the faith of the New Testament.

The unity of the Spirit (Eph. 4:2) is also a solemn warning to those who would advocate an organic union based on sacramentalism as a substitute for the spiritual unity which only the Spirit can give the body of Christ, the church. This ecclesiastical danger, however, should not be used as a shield for indifference to God's call to walk worthily "with all lowliness and meekness, with patience, forbearing one another in love, eager to maintain the unity of the Spirit in the bond of peace" (Eph. 4:2–3, RSV).

The ministry (*diakonia*) of the Spirit likewise may be summed up with three New Testament terms: the gifts (*charismata*) of the Spirit, the filling of the Spirit, the sword of the Spirit.

The gifts (*charismata*) of the Spirit are not the same as the gift (*dōrea*) of the Spirit, the first being what the Spirit gives and the second being the Spirit himself. The term *charisma*, found outside of Paul only in Philo (de leg. Alleg. iii, 30) and 1 Peter 4:10, describes the spiritual endowments bestowed by the Spirit for the ministry of the church (1 Cor. 1:7; 12:4, 9, 30 f.; Rom. 12:6; Eph. 4:11).

The filling of the Spirit, appears often in Acts (2:4; 4:8; 4:31; 6:3, 5; 7:55; 9:17; 11:24) and takes on a special significance in Ephesians 5:18 as Paul moves from the wisdom (5:15–17) of the Christian life to the power of the Christian life (5:18–20). Christians are to avoid drunkenness and debauchery by being filled with the Spirit, which enables them to address one another in psalms directed toward God, hymns directed toward Christ, and songs inspired by the Spirit. It was this spiritual fulness that led some observers at Pentecost to conclude that Spirit-filled men were "filled with new wine" (Acts 2:13), but this filling of the Spirit is the source of power in the worship and work of the Church.

The sword of the Spirit (Eph. 6:17) brings the nature of the church to a grand climax. The church pits herself against the world; and the Spirit with which she is filled, like a warrior, wields the living word of God until every power of darkness is vanquished (Heb. 4:12; Rev. 1:16; 2:16; 19:15, 21).

An exalted view of the living God leads to an exalted view of "the church of the living God, the pillar and ground of the truth" (1 Tim. 3:15, ASV). The mystery of godliness in Jesus Christ is the point from which to start both in the understanding of God and of "the household of God" (Eph. 2:19). The highest point in our understanding of God is reached in the formulation of the doctrine of the Holy Trinity, and it is from this perspective that the true nature of the church is revealed.

II

THE ORIGIN
OF THE CHURCH

R. W. Kicklighter

JESUS' ASSERTION THAT HE DID NOT COME "to destroy but to fulfill" applies to the church as well as the law; for the church, like other New Testament concepts, has its roots in the Old Testament. As L. S. Thornton states: "The new fellowship was born in the matrix of an older community, the old Israel." [1] An understanding of Jesus' declaration, "I will build my church," is dependent upon a grasp of the background of his thinking and intentions. Hence, an investigation of the origin of the church necessarily involves a study of the distinctly religious terms and concepts which existed in the mind of the New Testament writers.

The writers of the New Testament recognized a continuity of thought and development between the old and the new in the life and growth of the church. Stephen unhesitatingly applied the term "church" (*ekklēsia*) to the time of Moses, whom he declared "was in the church in the wilderness . . . with our fathers: who received the lively oracles to give unto us" (Acts 7:38). The writer of the book of Hebrews (2:12) quotes Psalm 22:22 as applying to the Messiah who there called the redeemed "my brethren" and said, "In the midst of the church will I sing praise unto thee." In a similar

[1] L. S. Thornton, *The Common Life in the Body of Christ* (3rd ed.; London: Dacre Press, 1950), p. 6.

28

manner Paul alluded to the Old Testament when he spoke of "the church of the Lord which he obtained with his own blood" (Acts 20:28). Hort has pointed out that if this is not a free quotation it is at least a clear echo of Psalm 74:2, which recalls the redeemed *edhah*, congregation, of the Exodus.[2] These references emphasize the existence of a close connection between the congregation of Israel in the Old Testament (Hebrew *qahal* or *edhah*, translated by the Septuagint as *ekklēsia*) and the New Testament use of *ekklēsia* to designate the Christian church.

Nothing so strengthens this continuity of thought and development as does the conviction of Paul that the early Christians were a "new creation" (humanity), "the Israel of God," or Peter's assertion that they were "an elect race, a royal priesthood, a holy nation, a people for God's own possession . . . the people of God." James felt free to address the church as "the twelve tribes which are of the dispersion." In Romans there is an extended treatment of "the large sweep of the history of the People of God from the time of Abraham, and the particular historical events which led to the emergence of the Christian Church." [3] The impetus of Pentecost in the origin of the church is, according to apostolic preaching, the result of the church's reception of the promised fellowship of the Spirit. The early church looked back to a definite and distinct background in the history of Israel as recorded in the Old Testament.

The New Testament term *ekklēsia* has Old Testament associations. Its classical and secular use carried the idea of "called out" and usually referred to a gathering of citizens

[2] Fenton John Anthony Hort, *The Christian Ecclesia* (London: Macmillan and Co., 1914), pp. 13–14.
[3] C. H. Dodd, *The Epistle of Paul to the Romans* ("Moffatt New Testament Commentary" New York: R. Long and R. R. Smith, Inc., 1932), p. xxxii.

called out from their homes into some public place for the purpose of deliberating. In the New Testament the word carries a distinct meaning, for in the Hebraic-Christian tradition *ekklēsia* was more than *an* assembly; it was *the* assembly. The use of the definite article with *ekklēsia* in Christian literature is an evidence of its exceptional nature and suggests a peculiar connotation, which must have made it somewhat meaningless to a contemporary Greek unfamiliar with Jewish or Christian practices. As Hoskyns and Davey point out, ". . . the phrase, *the ekklēsia*, used absolutely, though consistent in the New Testament, is never once found in secular writings." [4] Add to this the expression *ekklēsia tou theou* (the church of God), and more than classical or contemporary secular Greek is needed for comprehension.

The Septuagint Use of Ekklēsia

There was one book used by both Christians and Jews which employed the equivalent of this unique phrase. It was the Septuagint, the Bible of the early church. This Greek version of the Hebrew Scriptures was frequently used by the writers of the New Testament in quotation and allusion and is considered to be the only Bible known to most of the early Christians. More than half of the quotations from the Old Testament found in the New Testament are taken from the Septuagint.[5] It is also invaluable because "the Greek word in the Septuagint tends to carry the meaning of the original Hebrew word, and not its own meaning as a normal Greek word." [6] This applies especially to the dis-

[4] Sir Edwyn Hoskyns and Noel Davey, *The Riddle of the New Testament* (London: Faber & Faber, Ltd., 1936), p. 27.

[5] A. T. Robertson, *A Grammar of the Greek New Testament in the Light of Historical Research* (5th ed.; New York: Hodder and Stoughton, 1931), p. 99.

[6] Norman H. Snaith, *The Distinctive Ideas of the Old Testament* (Philadelphia: The Westminster Press, 1946), p. 205.

tinctly religious terms, including the Christian use of *ekklēsia*.

An investigation of the Septuagint use of *ekklēsia* includes a consideration of the Hebrew words *qahal* and *edhah* along with the related use of Greek *sunagōgē* to translate these two words. *Edhah* is used predominantly to refer to the whole congregation of Israel, assembled or unassembled, the society itself. Eighty-two per cent of the occurrences of this word are found in the Pentateuch, where it indicates in a technical sense the company of the Exodus. It is interesting to note that the Septuagint uses "Israel" to translate *edhah* in Numbers 4:34. This same use of *edhah* is observed in Psalm 74:2.

The root meaning of *qahal*, "to call together, to convoke," is similar to the Greek *ekklēsia*, and its most frequent use, like *edhah*, is with reference to the people of Israel, either as gathered in assembly or as constituting an organized community. It is used synonymously with *edhah* in Numbers 10:1-7 and 16:3 and in apposition with "all Israel" in 1 Chronicles 28:8. It carries the meaning of the term "nation" in the priestly law concerning the Day of Atonement for all Israel (Lev. 16:17-19, 29-34). Any local assembly of Israel convened for a specific purpose or absolute Israel, the unassembled community of God, was known as the *qahal* or *edhah*.

A numerical and historical study of the occurrences of these two words logically indicates that *qahal* gradually absorbed the meaning and use of *edhah* until, after the Exile, it was used almost exclusively for the assembly or congregation of Israel, whether assembled or absolute. Thus it became the more definite and formal word possessing a value judgment. The value judgment becomes explicit when the phrase reads *Yahweh qahal* (Yahweh's congregation), for this makes it emphatic that the community belonged to God and was his own peculiar possession. In the Pentateuch both words are translated *sunagōgē* by the Septuagint. However, from Deuteronomy 5:19 (22) on *ekklēsia* is the customary translation of *qahal*, and *sunagōgē* is reserved for *edhah*. The Hebrew *Yahweh qahal* became the Septuagint *ekklēsia kuriou* (congregation of the Lord), and this phrase furnishes the background of the New Testament *ekklēsia tou theou*. Hoskyns and Davey conclude that whatever their intention, the Septuagint translators "caused *ekklēsia of the Lord* to become a common scriptural phrase with exactly the same allusion to Israel's vocation as the *qahal of Jehovah*."[7] Surely the New Testament writers were aware of these definite associations.

Characteristics Common to Israel and the Church

Several recognizable features of this *Yahweh qahal* (congregation of Jehovah) are factors in the origin of the church and throw light upon the early church's consciousness of its distinctive nature.

The first characteristic is the element of *particularity* arising from the experience of election. This Hebrew knowledge of election was not speculative; it was based experientially upon God's redeeming activity. There was the memorable and concrete experience of the Exodus and Jehovah's further special acts of intervention which sustained God's people in a unique manner. The classic expression of the election of Israel is to be found in the Exodus experience where God explains that the delivered congregation was his peculiar possession, chosen only because of his redeeming love and not because of Israel's intrinsic worth (Deut. 7:6–9). God's initiative and elective choice of the nation is also implicit in the arbitrary selection of the patriarchs. This unique relationship

[7] Hoskyns and Davey, *op. cit.*, p. 29.

which existed between God and his people is described in terms of "sonship," which is an ethical relationship in which the divine initiative operated and Israel experienced God's love, protection, and discipline in a special way. Likewise the appellation "holy," as applied to Israel, emphasized the idea of distinctiveness. The people were "separate to" Jehovah as well as "separate from" the world in an ethical sense.

As the demands of holiness increased, the scope of particularity narrowed until election ultimately involved a righteous remnant. History discloses that the nation was unable to meet God's requirements of exclusive loyalty and absolute obedience. It was a remnant alone who kept the covenant and the faith alive. Seven thousand did not bend their knee to Baal in Elijah's day; a remnant listened to Isaiah and the prophets; a remnant made up "the saints" in Daniel and eventually returned from Babylon to restore the liturgical worship in Jerusalem; a remnant followed Judas Maccabeus. When Christ came, it was a remnant within Israel who believed in him. H. Wheeler Robinson has discriminatingly stated that "the rise of the doctrine of a righteous remnant . . . marks the future transference of religion from a nationalistic to an ecclesiastical basis." [8]

God's acts of deliverance, as in the Exodus, continued in the New Testament. It was his redemptive activity in Christ which gave birth to the church and is the basis for the Christian consciousness of particularity. Paul, a Christ-called apostle, wrote: "Unto the church of God which is at Corinth, even them that are sanctified in Christ Jesus, called to be saints, with all that call upon the name of our Lord Jesus Christ in every place, their Lord and ours" (1 Cor. 1:2). Paul, the members of the church at Corinth, and those every-

[8] H. Wheeler Robinson, *Inspiration and Revelation in the Old Testament* (Oxford: The Clarendon Press, 1946), p. 157.

where who share a similar experience *in Christ* are an "elect" and distinct people. Terms of distinction in the Old Israel are transferred to Christ's church and its members.

The appellation "saints," used interchangeably with *ekklēsia* in Paul's salutations to churches, is equivalent to the Septuagint "holy" and suggests the same idea of *separated from* the world and *separated to* God. Appeals to holy living are based on the holiness of God and the distinctiveness of the members of the community (2 Cor. 6:14 to 7:1; cf. 1 Pet. 2:1–16). Sonship, reserved in the Old Testament for elected Israel, became a process of "adoption" through Christ so that members of the Christian community were "heirs of God, and joint-heirs with Christ" (Rom. 8:14–17). They were now, through faith, the true sons of Abraham. The new basis of election in the new community was summed up "in Christ," that is, in the redemptive act of God, and was instrumental in the formation of the early church. *Ekklēsia*, from the compound verb *ek kaleō* meaning "to call out" is a fitting term of designation for this "separate" community.

The second characteristic to be noticed is the element of *mission* or service. If election is viewed alone or election to privilege is substituted for election to service, "the scandal of particularity" arises with its arbitrary selection of some individuals for salvation and others for damnation. However, privilege involves responsibility; election necessarily includes service. This principle is definite in the deliverance of the nation where Israel was given a mission. God ordered his people set free that they might serve him (Ex. 4:22; Deut. 7:6–9). Even the patriarchs had been favored that they might be a blessing to their children and all peoples (Gen. 9:8–11; 12:1–3; 28:3–4). God continually relented his fierce wrath toward his people in order that his name might be glorified, that is, that his true nature (Redeemer-God) might be manifest before all (1 Sam. 12:22; Isa. 48:9). The *saved* remnant of Ezekiel, the prototype of strict Judaism, must be evaluated in the light of the *saving* remnant of Isaiah, the prototype of evangelical Christianity. The exclusiveness of the remnant in Isaiah was for the purpose of worldwide evangelism. The remnant was to raise up the tribes of Jacob, restore the preserved of Israel, be a light to the Gentiles, and make known God's salvation to the end of the earth (Isa. 49:3–6; 42:6–7). Israel was chosen for the privilege of service. When election and service are united, "the scandal of particularity" is transformed into the glory of missionary activity. Israel lost this prophetic note, and Jesus redeemed it in the formation of his church.

The election of the Hebrew *qahal* was fundamentally for service, as was that of the New Testament *ekklēsia*. Christ called and commissioned disciples that he might "send them forth," even as the Father had sent him, to preach the good news of salvation. The exalted Christ left them with his worldwide mission (Matt. 28:19–20). The history of the church in Acts is the story of missionary activity whereby the gospel was carried from Jerusalem to Rome. The church had been constituted by Christ's proclamation of the gospel. Now, in extension, its very life was continued by the church's proclamation of this same gospel. The call of God in Christ is to the ministry of reconciliation (2 Cor. 5:14–20).

The disciples, as Christ's representatives, were to participate in his redemptive suffering (Matt. 20:22; Mark 10:38). Paul, deeply conscious of this union with Christ in redemptive suffering, declared: "Now I rejoice in my sufferings for your sake, and fill up on my part that which is lacking of the afflictions of Christ in my flesh for his body's sake, which is the church" (Col. 1:24, ASV).

This vicarious and redemptive mission of Christ has "overflowed" into the members of the church at Corinth as well as to Paul. Thus Paul could apply the language of the Suffering Servant to Christians. In Ephesians, where the church is pictured as the supernatural body of Christ, the theme is "the glory of the Christian movement in the Christian Church viewed as the progressive life of God in Christ reconciling the world unto himself." [9] The church is the messianic community elected for the purpose of sharing with Christ the messianic vocation of redemption. The church's consciousness of mission, founded upon the saving activity of God, is an impressive dynamic in the New Testament and a continuation of the original purpose of God. This dynamic motivation is an essential causative factor in the origin of the church.

In the third place, the sharing of an experience of redemptive election and a mission of service creates a sense of *fellowship*. This idea of fellowship is of two dimensions; the human and the divine-human. The vertical relationship (God with man) determines the horizontal relationship (man with man). This is observed in the basic religious unit in the Old Testament—the community or people of God. The covenant at Mount Sinai was made with the people as a group, and individuals shared the benefits of this covenant by virtue of membership in the redeemed community (Deut. 5:1–6). The new covenant of Jeremiah written in the hearts of men was still a covenant with "the house of Israel." The Exodus was a community project. The prerequisite of the individual responsibility in the Passover was the fact of belonging to a special people. When God brought his people out of Egypt, he delivered them as the "children of Israel" rather than as individuals. It was this Exodus experience which "made them

[9] William Owen Carver, *The Glory of God in the Christian Calling* (Nashville: Broadman Press, 1949), p. 5.

a free people, with an ideal of solidarity that overrode the instinctive selfishness of individual and clan." [10] Isaiah's remnant, Jeremiah's new covenant, Ezekiel's new community of the Spirit, and Daniel's "saints of the Most High" were all expressions of a future hope that involved people as a group. The social unit emphasized the idea of fellowship on a common level.

This sense of togetherness can be seen in Israel's social morality. Both blessings and punishment traversed the modern "individual-society" distinction. Descendants were blessed because of the righteousness of ancestors, children were visited with the iniquities of the fathers, and the sin of one brought punishment upon many. The sense of community was so strong that the individual could be identified with the group or vice versa. The people of God belonged together because they belonged to God.

The determining factor in this consciousness of a close human relationship was the knowledge of an intimate experience with God. The adhesive quality of this unique community was the immediate presence of Almighty God in their midst. Israel believed in the immanence of her God because she had experienced his direct control of history. He participated in her every activity and experience. The Exodus was followed by many other divine acts of redemption and intervention. The children of Israel were conscious of God's presence at the center of their life. The ark was a symbol and guarantee of his presence. Both God and man participated in the act of sacrifice. The Temple, filled with his burning presence, stood as a constant reminder that God was tabernacling in their midst. God was active and present; they were his people; they belonged together in a unique sense.

[10] C. H. Dodd, *The Authority of the Bible* (New York: Harper & Brothers, 1929), p. 46.

In the New Testament a similar cohesive bond is noted. As has been observed, Christian election is founded upon an experience of salvation "in Christ" for the purpose of sharing with him in his messianic suffering and redemptive enterprise. The unifying bond in the Christian fellowship is an awareness of a vertical relationship to the God who has entered history in the person of Jesus Christ. The divine component is observed in the experience of Pentecost, which is the expressed result of the activity of the Holy Spirit. This influx of the supernatural at Pentecost resulted in the formation of a unique human fellowship. After the descent of the Holy Spirit, the followers of Christ "continued stedfastly in the apostles' teaching and [in the] fellowship [*koinōnia*], in the breaking of bread and the prayers" (Acts 2:42, ASV). The use of the article with *koinōnia* distinguishes it from the apostles' teaching and indicates that the disciples were occupied constantly with four distinct activities, of which the *koinōnia*, the fellowship, was one.

The word *koinōnia* represents one of the predominant ideas of the New Testament. From the verb meaning "to have a share in," "to come into communion," or "to come into fellowship" it also signified participation or partnership. The dominant meaning is "an interior spiritual reality, an activity of sharing or communion, constituting an inner bond of that brotherly concord which, in turn, is realized and expressed in the life of the community." [11] Sharing in the divine Gift and experiencing an inner fellowship, it was quite natural for the early Christians to share spontaneously their material possessions. The *koinōnia* of Acts 2:42 resulted in the Christians' having all things common (*koinos*) in Acts 2:44. Here is a unique human fellowship instigated and governed by the Holy Spirit.

[11] Thornton, *op. cit.*, p. 451.

Both horizontal and vertical fellowship are involved in the observance of the Lord's Supper. The purpose of Paul's instructing the Corinthians concerning the Lord's Supper was to correct divisions which existed in the fellowship when they came together "in the church" (1 Cor. 11:16-20). The act of participating in the Lord's Supper was an expression of human fellowship which was central in the life of the early church. The lack of *koinōnia* between men was a denial of *koinōnia* with God. Paul preceded his rebuke of the rupture of human sharing with an explanation of the nature and significance of the Lord's Supper, in which the participants have communion (*koinōnia*) with Christ (10:16-17). Unbrotherly action violated God's presence. The early church life was an expression of vertical and horizontal fellowship in which the bond of union between the members was the consciousness of a common relationship to God who was vividly present.

This sense of community extended beyond the bounds of the local situation. In the previously quoted salutation of Paul to the church at Corinth the members there were "called to be saints, with all that call upon the . . . Lord Jesus Christ in every place, their Lord and ours" (1 Cor. 1:2 ASV). The members of this local church were related to the members of other churches where the same activity of God in Christ was manifest in a similar manner. It was this spirit which motivated the collection, called a *koinōnia*, which Paul secured from the Gentile churches for the poverty-stricken church at Jerusalem (Rom. 15:26, 2 Cor. 8:4). The expression, organization, and government of the New Testament churches was local in nature, but there was an emphasized unity of the spirit which makes the attitudes and distinctions developed in the denominational history of the church somewhat foreign to the life and spirit of the New Testament era. As E. F. Scott states:

There was no set ministry, for the gifts of the Spirit were bestowed upon all; no stated mode of worship, for the Spirit moved as it listed and its impulses must not be quenched; no formal scheme of doctrine, which might exclude the new revelations imparted from time to time by the Spirit. The scattered groups of Christians were not confederated by any outward ties; together they made up the church, in which dwelt the one Spirit, and no other bond of union was deemed necessary.[12]

The church in its origin was a living organism of the Spirit rather than an organization of ecclesiastical institutionalism. In it the consciousness of togetherness was exceptionally strong.

The unity of the church, conceived of as the body of Christ, is difficult to understand in terms of a human institution. Irrespective of size or grouping, the church is a group of disciples plus the presence of Christ and the Spirit of Christ, which is the cohesive factor. Since Christ and his Spirit are possessed by one and all alike, the unity of the part and the whole is established. Thus Hoskyns and Davey conclude:

The word [ekklēsia] has been transformed [in Christ] to denote a body of men and women in which the unity of every part corresponds to, repeats, represents, and in fact is the unity of the whole. . . . The part is equal to the whole, because each part possesses, not a fragment of the Christ, but the whole Christ, and consequently, in accordance with the mathematical definition, the ekklēsia is of the order of infinity.[13]

The church is a qualitative organism rather than a quantitative organization. In the words of Paul, "This mystery is great: but I speak in regard of Christ and of the church" (Eph. 5:32).

[12] Ernest F. Scott, *The Beginnings of the Church* (New York: Charles Scribner's Sons, 1914), p. 78.
[13] Hoskyns and Davey, *op. cit.*, p. 32.

The New Element

The church in its origin was distinguished by three dominant characteristics: particularity, mission, and fellowship. All three characteristics are rooted in the Old Testament and are a continuation of the purpose and people of God. But the *ekklēsia* of the New Testament cannot be understood solely in terms of the Old Testament. To do so would be to interpret the church simply as a sect within Judaism no different from the groups of disciples that gathered around outstanding religious teachers; the Judaizers made this mistake. The decisive and determining factor in the New Testament church is Christ Jesus. The election or calling is in and through him. The mission is a participation in his messianic redemption. The fellowship is a sharing of his nature. Christ is the head of his church, the dominant and constitutive element in the church, possessed by one and all alike. Apart from him there can be no Christian church. Christ is so responsible for the foundation and life of the church that Paul unhesitatingly wrote, "All the churches of Christ salute you" (Rom. 16:16).

The church is the new creation of Christ. Paul spoke of the "one new man," or humanity, which Christ created of Jew and Gentile, that he might "reconcile them both in one body unto God" (Eph. 2:15–16). Because of this new creation, the Gentiles who were "separate from Christ, alienated from the commonwealth of Israel, and strangers from the covenants of the promise" were now "made nigh in the blood of Christ" (Eph. 2:12–13). The term "body" and the metaphors found in this passage are used elsewhere in this book and in Paul's writing to refer to the church. Therefore, it is logical to conclude that the concept of the new humanity created by Christ may be identified with the church. The church is Christ's body and is constituted by him to do his work on earth.

The historical events which initiated the establishment of the Christian church were Christ's ministry and the apostolic proclamation at Pentecost that "God hath made him both Lord and Christ." R. Newton Flew has correctly concluded, "The Christian Church was constituted by this apostolic conviction that Jesus was Messiah, and exalted to the right hand of God." [14] Emil Brunner marks the beginning of the history of the church with the mystery of Pentecost and states, "The outpouring of the Holy Ghost and the existence of the *Ecclēsia* are so closely connected that they may be actually identified." [15] The incredible progress and formal organization of the church as recorded in Acts was the result of the leadership and possession of the Holy Spirit who was given to the church community by the exalted Christ. Both by creative act and sustaining life, Christ was the chief cornerstone upon which the spiritual house was being built.

The Church in Christ's Purpose

This investigation has now reached the point that an examination of Jesus' intention to form an exclusive community is in order. It has been doubted by some that Jesus ever intended to found an exclusive church separate from Israel. Advocates of this view have held that Jesus had come preaching "the kingdom of God," and Paul and the apostles afterward converted this gospel into an ecclesiastical program. The fact that only the Gospel of Matthew indicates that Christ used the term *ekklēsia* (and only twice, at that) is considered added justification for this view. Textual criticism is

[14] R. Newton Flew, *Jesus and His Church* (2nd ed.; London: The Epworth Press, 1951), p. 161.

[15] *The Misunderstanding of the Church*, trans. Harold Knight (Philadelphia: The Westminster Press, 1953), p. 11.

unable to remove these two utterances, since there are no known Greek manuscripts or ancient versions which lack Matthew 16:18. If it can be shown that Christ actually intended a community of the nature of the *ekklēsia*, then one of the main objections to Jesus' infrequent use of the term will be answered. Limits of space necessitate a brief survey statement without full discussion.

Several basic themes, central in Christ's teaching and activity, imply the formation of an *ekklēsia*. First, the gospel phrase "the kingdom of God"—the redemptive rule of God in action—does not operate in a void. It necessarily involves a community of subjects among whom this activity of reigning is exercised. The parable of the mustard seed, if interpreted in the light of Daniel 4:14 and Ezekiel 31:3, 6, makes clear the formation of a community in the kingdom concept. To be a disciple was the equivalent of entering into the kingdom. The disciples, the nucleus of the early church, followed Christ in view of his proclamation of the arrival of the kingdom of God. The actual result of the gospel was the formation of the church.

The second proposal is that the idea of messiahship, also central in the life and teachings of Christ, envisages the formation of a community of believers. The title "Son of man," Jesus' term of self-designation, is a messianic title (cf. Dan. 7:13–27). When Jesus was asked by the high priest if he were "the Christ, the Son of the Blessed," he answered by quoting from Daniel 7:13. Here Christ identified the Son of man and the Messiah by referring to a passage which speaks of the resultant community of "the people of the saints of the Most High." Jesus, also, was the first to identify the Son of man and the Suffering Servant of Isaiah (Mark 8:31; 9:9, 12, 31; 10:33, 45; 14:21, 41; Luke 22:48, 69; 24:7). In Isaiah 53 the sufferings of the Servant were to be a ransom for many, that is, for a group or community. The concept of the Messiah as a Shepherd is applied to Christ and involves a flock (Mark 15:37; John 10:14–16). It is interesting to note that Paul referred to the church as "the flock" and instructed the elders from Ephesus "to feed the church of the Lord" (Acts 20:28). These messianic categories, all applied to Christ, are incomplete unless there is a corresponding and resultant community.

Jesus translated these ideals into reality during his ministry. Near the beginning of his ministry he called twelve apostles or disciples. The act of calling men to leave all and follow him is positive proof that Jesus intended the establishment of a society. The number twelve, corresponding to the number of tribes of Israel, is significant. Hort declared that "whenever we find disciples and discipleship . . . there we are dealing with what was a direct preparation for the founding of the Ecclesia." [16] Jesus appointed the twelve for a dual purpose: first, that they should have fellowship with him; and second, that he might send them forth (Mark 3:14–15). The Greek conjunction separating the two purposes makes the calling and fellowship point to the sending forth or mission of making other disciples, that is, the formation of a society. Jesus also established a covenant with the twelve at the Last Supper. This covenant, reminiscent of the Old Testament covenant at Mount Sinai, is clarified by the covenants of Isaiah 43:6–7 and 49:8–9 where the Servant is given for "a covenant with the people." This brief survey is sufficient to show that Jesus intended the formation of an exclusive, missionary community, and its formation has been shown to be the direct result of his Person and ministry.

Since Jesus intended the establishment of the church, it is reasonable to allow him the use of the term *ekklēsia* or its equivalent. It is generally accepted that Christ probably spoke

[16] Hort, *op. cit.*, pp. 19–20.

Aramaic when he said, "I will build my church." [17] If such be the case, then Christ probably used the Aramaic equivalent for the Hebrew *qahal*, and Matthew recognized the close association of the Hebrew *qahal* and *ekklēsia* in the Septuagint. With these considerations in mind, Hort wrote, "If we may venture for a moment to substitute the name Israel, and read the words as 'on this rock I will build my Israel . . . we gain an impression which supplies at least an approximation to the probable sense." [18] Perhaps Hort would have been nearer correct if he had used the word *qahal* instead of Israel. The ministry and teachings of Jesus furnish sufficient evidence to warrant the conclusion that Jesus intended the formation of a society which embodies the idea of the church. The development of this ideal in its formal organization and concrete expression is another question which cannot be dealt with in the limits of this discussion.

This approach to the origin of the church recognizes God's historically revealed purpose in establishing his unique messianic community, elective in nature, active in divine service, and animated by his Spirit. The early church's consciousness of its connection with the past is acknowledged. The climax and glory of this development is revealed to be in Christ, who makes all things new. He is seen to be the originating and sustaining factor in the Christian church, which is new because of him. Ultimately the origin of the church is to be found in him.

[17] John A. Broadus, *Commentary on the Gospel of Matthew* (Philadelphia: American Baptist Publication Society, 1886), p. 355 ff.
[18] Hort, *op. cit.*, pp. 10-11.

III

THE MINISTRY IN THE
NEW TESTAMENT
CHURCHES

S. A. Newman

THE PRESENT GENERATION has turned to a re-examination of
Christian antiquity with the hope of finding new light on
problems of twentieth-century ecclesiology, attempting to
determine what those closest to the fountainhead of Christian
faith meant by what they said and did.

Baptists are always encouraged by any indication of interest in New Testament history. Popularly they have expressed
their historical premise by a simple formula: Whatever can
be learned about the beliefs and practices of the first generation of disciples must be followed conscientiously.

Why did the earliest disciples act as they did in the conduct
of their Christian affairs? It is evident that they did not act
solely to provide a detailed example for later Christian generations to follow. Their conduct was rather the effect of
dynamic faith operating within their own Christian situation.
Thus a valid distinction can be made between what they did
to meet the needs of their time and the timeless principles
that guided their actions. The ideas and usages of every generation of Christians should be determined, both as to nature and worth, *by the genius of the religion from which they
flow.*

This study is not, therefore, an attempt to recover a fragment of history; the primary consideration is not history but doctrine. The examination of the details of history will reveal no set of practices which, per se, lie as an obligation on Christians today. Instead, insight into that original historical situation discloses the manner and conduct of persons caught up in the quality of the Christian religion; it becomes invaluable in its relevance in so far as Christians now seek to become equally involved in the same religion.

What the church is and what its nature obligates it to do give meaning and value to the services of its members. The nature of the ministry is inherent in the nature of the church, and the nature of the church is inherent in the genius of Christian faith. Thus study of the earliest aspects of the Christian ministry involves study of the functioning church in the first century.

The real differences of opinion among contemporary Christians regarding the ministry in the first century, therefore, are due to differences regarding the inherent quality and consequent purposes of Christianity. The problem is not a lack of agreement merely about the details of the historical situation but about their theological significance.

The necessity for interpreting historical details is further complicated by the fact that evidently there was no single, consistent pattern of church life in the apostolic era. For example, it is instructive for those who subscribe to congregational democracy to recall, in the language of McNutt, "that every other denomination of Christian people has likewise found the roots of its polity in this same New Testament." [1] There is language suggestive of episcopal and of presbyterial as well as of congregational practice in the church life of the earliest generation of believers.

[1] William R. McNutt, *Polity and Practice of Baptist Churches* (Philadelphia: The Judson Press, 1935), p. 10.

This fact determines the choice of method for the study of the ministry in the first century. Rather than search for a fixed, detailed pattern, it is necessary to define as clearly as possible the principles which lie behind the whole order of the "churchly" in Christianity and observe how the first disciples employed these principles in the administration of their church affairs.

The Church of the First Disciples

The New Testament record presents two facts: the existence of the church within the social situation of the first century and within that church the functioning of a ministry which seems to have been recognized as in some sense official. It is necessary to recognize, however, that there was development in practice within the New Testament period.

A church with no formal organization.—Trying to reconstruct the situation of the original believers indicates that they had

no formal organization at all; it is the creative power of the religious experience centered in Jesus Christ spontaneously influencing the emergence of the 'ecclesiai'. . . . Eye-witnesses, fresh from their contacts with Jesus, spake what they had seen and heard; the spiritual elements embodied in them through such contacts awoke a response; the seed of the gospel was taking root in good ground, the communities of believers were showing themselves.[2]

"They were originally simple fraternities of pious faith and life, whose members knew the equality of all as spiritual men and saints . . . and brothers one to another. There were no offices with peculiar privileges, only the voluntary services,

[2] P. G. S. Hopwood, *The Religious Experience of the Primitive Church* (New York: Charles Scribner's Sons, 1937), p. 211.

which established a moral demand for grateful recognition and subordination of others." [3]

A sense of unique relationship to Jesus Christ.—Through his ministry, Jesus carefully planted his teachings in the lives of his hearers. He was able to inspire a growing sense of relation between his followers and himself. He was a creative, energizing influence in the total experience of his devotees. This was so transforming as to be interpreted by them as a complete spiritual re-orientation; they had been overtaken by the "Eternal." Their conduct was motivated by a high order of ethical consciousness; they were "new creatures in Christ Jesus." This revolutionary involvement produced in them a confident mutuality which at once separated them from all others and at the same time bound them into a group recognizable as a Christian fellowship.

As Neander has succinctly described it, "The first Christian community formed as it were one family; the power of the newly awakened . . . fellowship, the feeling of the common grace of redemption, outweighed all other . . . feelings, and all other relations were subordinated to this one great relation." [4]

From spontaneity to organization.—It has been insistently suggested by several that the spiritual orientation of the original group was completely eschatological in character. If this view could be proved correct, such faith could be understood in the light of the overwhelming implications of Jesus' impact upon the first disciples. Hopwood has taken this extreme position.[5] He interpreted the pure form of responsive discipleship to have been maintained on an altogether "other-

---

[3] Otto Pfleiderer, *Christian Origins,* trans. Daniel A. Huebsch (New York: B. W. Huebsch, 1906), p. 281.

[4] A. Neander, *History of the Planting and Training of the Christian Church* (London: Henry G. Bohn, 1859), I, 23.

[5] *Op. cit.,* pp. 246 ff.

worldly" basis, with no regard for time or place. When its
eschatological expectation was not immediately fulfilled, he
insisted, the early church then turned to the mundane aspects
of historical existence. Thus the church—as an institutionali-
zation of the originally spontaneous fellowship—was born in
what this author termed "the grand failure." For him there
was a retrogression, a dilution of the purest form of Christian
life when the group became externalized enough to require
modes of operation such as are needed by other social institutions.

Without accepting all this, it is still necessary to make a distinction between the church in ideal existence and the church
in actual historical relationships. The development of organization within the church carried with it a sort of embryonic
ecclesiasticism. The appearance of the "official" who is
thought of as occupying a "position" came at a time when
the fellowship had acquired an element which was not to be
found in its essential form, and something which in many respects stood in contradiction to the original character of the
church. One cannot ascribe a qualitative difference to officers
as over against the "ordinary" members of the church without making the persons who occupy those offices necessary
means of grace. This danger implicit in officialdom was not
recognized at the time, for first-century Christianity consistently held to the gospel as the only necessity for satisfactory
religious experience.

Prominence through service.—Jesus had appeared in the
role of preacher and teacher, and those who came within the
creative circle of his presence used preaching and teaching to
share with others what they had known of him. This proclamation of the Christian message was so important to those
who heard it that they came to give a certain prominence to
the persons who thus witnessed. These were acknowledged

as having been providentially commissioned (apostled) for such service.

In their conscientious devotion, the first Christian leaders thought of themselves as having a commission to bridge the gap between the personal presence of Jesus and the generation which had not known him in the flesh. It is in this sense alone that the apostolic ministry stands apart from the congregation of believers. Viewed from this angle, it is legitimate to interpret it, with Schaff and many others, as being of divine origin, greatness, and dignity. It is not surprising that eventually there came to be a chasm between the apostles and the people, an "opposition of clergy and laity," to use modern terms. In that sense the "office is not, indeed, a creature of the congregation. It is itself the creative beginning of the church, the divinely appointed organ of her establishment and edification." [6]

In continuing this line of thought, however, Schaff moved dangerously near the *faux pas* of historical Christianity. He contended that the apostles themselves, "as living persons in their union with Christ, and as organs of the Holy Ghost, are called the foundation of this spiritual edifice."

Schaff's language in its context is an approximation of that point of view which confuses a person with the ministry that that person performs. It overlooks the fact that in a real sense the first believers, the apostles themselves, were created by the identical process of which they became agents in creating the church.

Schaff felt constrained to modify the apparent implications of his definition by adding promptly:

But as soon as the gospel had taken root and produced a Christian community, there arose a relationship of active co-operation

[6] Philip Schaff, *History of the Apostolic Church* (New York: Charles Scribner's Sons, 1856), pp. 506 ff.

between pastor and people. Though the pastors retained control, yet they exercised it in the spirit of brotherly love and with the consciousness that the members of the flock stood essentially in the same relationship with themselves to the common Head and chief Shepherd, Jesus Christ; that they were sanctified by the same Spirit and had an equal share in all the privileges and blessings of salvation. . . . While on the other hand the churches were far from assuming authority over their leaders and were instructed to yield them affectionate obedience (Heb. 13:17; 1 Cor. 16:16).

Apostles irreplaceable eyewitnesses.—The apostles were prominent persons, but their prominence was not of the same order as has been described by much of subsequent Christian history. They were not infallible; they found it expedient to consult with each other regarding the meaning of what they had heard Jesus say and with reference to its application to the infinitely varied human situation.

They were an irreplaceable band, filling a unique place in the continuity of faith from Jesus to later generations. They were qualified as eyewitnesses, a position described as undemocratic by Brunner in his work, *The Misunderstanding of the Church.*[7] Thus the very thing that made them significant was not something that could be passed around to other Christians or handed to one's successors. What the apostles learned as eyewitnesses they shared with others by their witnessing, but others could not thereby be made to become eyewitnesses.

The writings which became the New Testament are the documentary account of the experiences of these eyewitnesses and of those closely associated with them. Therefore, with the passing of the apostolic generation, the New Testament writings became the accepted norm of truth concerning Jesus Christ. With the passing of the last of the apostles, the apostolic witness did not pass away. In a real sense the New

[7] *Op. cit.,* p. 25.

Testament is the apostolic authority for all subsequent generations.

Postapostolic Leadership

The achievement of a ministry of prominence and "authority" after the apostolic generation can be seen in the process by which the church came to be. It is equally revealing of many characteristics of leadership to investigate *what the church began to do* in the early years of its existence.

The work and the workers.—Lindsay has suggested that there were three fairly distinct kinds of work to which the church gave itself, in addition to its task of evangelistic or missionary endeavor. Each congregation carried on with some regularity a program of worship, edification, and what may be called "business." [8] With some allowance for overlapping functions, particular phases of Christian work came to be identified with the persons who customarily performed those services. In most cases the persons become "officers"; the services they rendered were crystallized into the categories of the ministry.

The principle by which the qualified would come to be singled out for special consideration was recognized by Jesus when he said, "He that is greatest among you shall be your servant" (Matt. 23:11). This junction of service with leadership, everywhere set forth in the New Testament, is associated with a third quality called "gifts." "The qualifications which fit a man for service and therefore for rule within the Church of Christ are always looked upon as special 'gifts' of the Spirit of God, or *charismata*." [9]

Worship leaders.—In Christianity as in any religion, the act

[8] T. M. Lindsay, *The Church and the Ministry in the Early Centuries* (Grand Rapids: Zondervan Publishing House, 1924), pp. 44 ff.
[9] *Ibid.*, p. 63.

of worship is near the heart of the faith. "It is through worship that man becomes conscious of God, that he brings his own life into relation with the divine life." [10] At the center of the corporate experience of the new Christian community was its worship of Jesus Christ.

It would be correct to insist that this Object of Christian worship was the unique element in the religious services of the early disciples. These had not come into their new religious way of life from a religious vacuum. Most of them were devout members of the Jewish community and faithful attendants upon its synagogue services of worship. The synagogue service was simple. It usually consisted of three parts: "reading of the Scriptures, in which God spoke to man; prayer and praise, in which man spoke to God; an address, in which man spoke to his fellow man." [11]

E. F. Scott stands almost alone in his interpretation of the influence of the Jewish background on the predominantly Jewish Christian church. While admitting considerable carry-over in the major aspects of the worship service, this author held that the church was not too directly influenced by the synagogue.

Instead of copying the Jewish institutions they adopted new ones, springing out of the inherent nature of their new faith. Nothing is more remarkable than this independence. . . . Perhaps it was due in some measure to the very fact that the disciples continued to be Jews, practicing the old along with their own. They did not need to devise some equivalent for the Law and the priesthood and the ritual, for in their Jewish faith they had all these things already. Their whole mind was devoted to the discovery of what was required of them by their new beliefs, and they were able to build up the church with a splendid freedom.

[10] E. F. Scott, *The Nature of the Early Church* (New York: Charles Scribner's Sons, 1941), p. 70.
[11] *Ibid.*, p. 72.

It was not the Jewish community over again, with a few minor differences, but was a new creation.[12]

There is a relevance which is convincing in this kind of argument, in view of the fact that the first Jewish converts did continue as active participants in their synagogues. They maintained their connections until their new faith made them so conspicuous among their Jewish fellows that they were forcibly expelled. It was not until they were required to discontinue their Jewish religious associations that they began to realize the sufficiency of their new faith as a separate religious system. When they could no longer attend the Jewish rites, they discovered how little they really needed anything that worship in a synagogue or the Jerusalem Temple could offer them.

In spite of this, the transfer of the form of group life from the old to the new, particularly in the leadership of worship, was almost complete. The synagogue had its council of "old men," qualified by years in knowledge and wisdom, who presided and performed the rituals of worship. It is not surprising, therefore, that the term "elder" appears as a natural designation in a casual reference to the leadership of the Jerusalem church. These recognized leaders were the ones to whom the funds for the needy should be dispatched (Acts 11:20), and they also would serve in the distribution of those funds. From the earliest times they stood to preside in the Christian assembly. Some of them read the Scriptures while others led in prayers, benedictions, songs, and the delivery of the hortatory discourse.

The man who stands regularly to lead worship will naturally receive a respect akin to reverence from those who worship with him. His esteem will be limited only by the effec-

[12] *Ibid.*, p. 31.

tiveness of his service and the degree of satisfaction others derive from it.

From the Jewish background and from functions within the fellowship there evidently emerged a group of leaders called "elders" (presbyters). Titles such as "pastor," "teacher," and "ruler" (bishop) could easily have come into use as terms descriptive of specialized activities within the group of elders.

Overseers of business.—It is reasonable to conclude that it was in the area of the "business" interests of the congregation that leaders came to be called "bishops" (*episkopoi,* literally, "overseers"). About the rise and growth of that office, however, there is far from universal agreement. The thesis of Lightfoot, with which many agree, was that originally the terms "bishop" and "presbyter" were identical. He concluded that "the episcopate was not formed out of the Apostolic order by localization, but out of the presbyterial by elevation; and the title, which originally was common to all, came at length to be appropriated to the chief among them." [13]

Evidence from surprising quarters indicates that episcopacy—in the later meaning of the term—was unknown to the "ruling elders" of the first-century church. No less authority of the Catholic tradition than Jerome (*ca.* A.D. 420) taught that the terms "bishop" and "elder" were synonymous in New Testament usage, that they referred to men of equal authority, and that the placing of the bishop above the presbyter was an ecclesiastical arrangement which was made in consequence of schism and other disorders within the church. [14]

Many have pointed out that while the office of elder is of

[13] Quoted by A. V. G. Allen, *Christian Institutions* (New York: Charles Scribner's Sons, 1910), p. 19.
[14] Cf. *Ibid.,* p. 6.

Hebrew origin, the term "bishop" is applied in the New Testament only to officers in Gentile churches though it did not supersede the use of the word "elder" even here. Timothy at Ephesus and Titus in Crete were performing what might be called episcopal functions as they ordained, encouraged, and reproved leadership in the churches; yet the New Testament does not refer to them as bishops. McGiffert has suggested that if the term might be applied legitimately to any individual of the apostolic age, it would seem that that individual would be James.[15] Yet New Testament sources do not warrant the use of the term with reference to him.

From occurrences of the term in the extant literature of the second century, it seems that the office of bishop was only occasionally recognized during the first half of that period and that it was not until near the close of the century that churches throughout the Roman Empire gave the office fairly general acknowledgment.

Practical considerations also gave rise in the church to the work of the "servants"—*diakonoi*, a term used of servants generally. As the work of ministering to the needy became large, the leaders of the Jerusalem church sought release from this for fuller devotion to "the ministry of the word." Interested and qualified persons were asked to engage in the ministry of "help." Though the term "deacon" (that is, "servant") does not occur in the passage, the circumstances recounted in Acts 6 undoubtedly describe the origin of the office.

In instructing Timothy, Paul gave in detail the qualities expected of those who were to serve as deacons, but he neglected to state the exact nature of their duties. It may not be purely incidental that the term is found in its feminine form

---

[15] A. C. McGiffert, *A History of Christianity in the Apostolic Age* (Edinburgh: T. & T. Clark, 1897), p. 554.

in some places in the New Testament record (cf. Rom. 16:1).

Leaders in edification.—The second type of work described by Lindsay was edification. Much that occupied the interests of the Christian assemblies had to do with what New Testament writers called "spiritual gifts," the *charismata*.[16] Specific mention is made of the gifts of prophecy, miracles, tongues, and "words of wisdom," as well as other kinds of gifts that were not so directly related to instruction.

Prominent among those possessing gifts, probably next to the apostles in the planting and edification of the churches, were those with the gift of prophecy. There is good evidence that the primary ability of prophets was to "tell forth," rather than to "fore tell." This was a providential expedient for the infant community at a time of paucity of authentic tradition. Apparently there was a decline in the prevalence of this gift among the churches as the New Testament writings became increasingly available.

In some instances these gifts meant individual capacities laid hold on, strengthened, vivified, and applied by the Spirit to service within the community. In others it was obviously the continuation of the type of supernaturalism which seems to have been given to the early disciples as a pledge and guarantee of identity with Jesus Christ—at a time when such corroboration was invaluable.

The ministry of gifts was liable to abuse, as is evidenced by the extreme condition which existed in the church at Corinth. Their exhibition, without the undergirding of genuine faith and the spirit of love, made them occasions of confusion and harm.

As other types of ministry became better established and were taken to be the normal procedure for Christian leadership, the exercise of gifts was disparaged and regarded as ir-

16 Cf. Schaff, *op. cit.*, p. 489, and Lindsay, *op. cit.*, pp. 71 ff.

regular. Paul seems to have been rising to the defense of the legitimate exercise of spiritual gifts when he warned the Thessalonians, "Quench not the Spirit" (1 Thess. 5:19).

Christian leaders thus endued were not responsible for having been given the *charismata;* they were responsible for the spirit and purpose in which the gifts were exercised. Such leaders were not appointed to formal offices, and women as well as men were thus endued for service in the upbuilding of the church.

Christian service as a vocation.—One additional suggestion must be made regarding the relationship of a "church" ministry and the first-century sense of vocation.

To the earliest disciples the lordship of Jesus Christ was taken to be universal, and they looked forward in the confidence that Christ's sovereignty would eventually be complete. Personal loyalty was without equivocation in all areas of experience, and Christian vocation was interpreted to mean the vocation engaged in by a Christian.

Within the historical circumstance into which the movement was thrust this pristine point of view was short-lived. There was the realistic problem of engaging upon Christian fellowship within the context of a non-Christian environment, with the added responsibility of mission to the unbelieving world. Some distinctions seemed to be necessary. Some things were known to be "sacred" (that is, "set apart" for God), and over against the sacred was the recalcitrant, pagan world. Here God's rights were not recognized, and everyday concerns, including work, were carried on by people who had no sense of the sacredness of life's activities. Gradually, but definitely, service in and for the church came to be identified with the sacred, and the results of that appraisal gave "secular" (that is, "belonging to the world") value to all other labor. Thus Christianity came to be robbed of one of its greatest glories, the sense of stewardship of all of life and its corollary, the dignity of work. From an early period there came to be reserved for the few who engaged in the immediate activities of the church the privilege of doing the will of the Lord; for the larger body of Christians there remained only the drab prospect of secular vocation.

Conclusion

When viewed in its historical context, it is not surprising that the church did not have a uniform pattern of polity and practice. The influence of current Jewish customs made leadership by elders the normal pattern for the new community. Likewise, there is every reason to believe that there was strong influence from Greek ideas and from the administrative example of civil magistracy, tending toward supervision by individual leaders. In the life of the infant community such tendencies toward centralized leadership by elders (presbyterial government) or individual overseers (episcopal government) were legitimate and constructive.

But there also was from the beginning a generous provision for the essential democracy of the fellowship which is implicit in the religion itself. Congregational polity appears along with the other forms, and there can be seen a gravitation toward this form when Christian beliefs receive their fullest expression in the functions of the community.

Few ideas are more demonstrable than that changes were made in the basic beliefs of Christianity during the course of its history. These changes in doctrine took place under forms of organization, including types of official leadership, which came in from sources outside the religion. It would seem to be more than a matter of coincidence that these changes were, in the main, modifications of belief to accommodate the presence of an "official" group within the Christian fellowship.

A ministry of "servants," recognized for the services they rendered rather than for the position they occupied, represents the purest forms of the ministry in the early church. This is the only form of ministry which is consonant with the essential character of Christian faith.

IV

THE DOCTRINE OF BAPTISM IN THE NEW TESTAMENT

T. C. Smith

ALL PROFESSING CHRISTIANS undergo some type of baptism, but this does not mean that all agree on the meaning of the baptism to which they submit. The past fifteen years have seen a great revival of interest on the subject of baptism. Scholars in Great Britain and on the Continent have called for a re-examination of the theology and practice of the rite within their own communions. Some have maintained that their communions were following the New Testament at all points, while others have broken with the teaching of their churches regarding baptism. H. G. Marsh, a Methodist, led the way in England with his book, *The Origin and Significance of the New Testament Baptism*, which was first published in 1940. In 1943 the eminent theologian, Karl Barth, delivered a lecture on baptism at a gathering of Swiss theological students, and the conclusions were shocking to many of the students and equally disturbing to Barth's colleagues in the University of Basle. Barth rejected the practice of infant baptism and claimed that believer's baptism was the only valid baptism. This lecture was first published in pamphlet form in 1946 under the title *Die Kirchliche Lehre von der Taufe* and was translated into English in 1948 by E. A. Payne, secretary of the British Baptist Missionary Society.

About the same time that Barth's pamphlet appeared,

Franz J. Leenhardt, professor of the University of Geneva, published a pamphlet entitled *Le Baptême Chrétien*. Leenhardt admitted that there was a lack of evidence in the New Testament for a defense of infant baptism, but he tried to set forth a way of understanding infant baptism which was not absolutely contrary to the true idea of baptism. His defense was vulnerable at all points. Also in 1946 an Anglican monk, Dom Gregory Dix, delivered a lecture at Oxford University which was later published under the title, *The Theology of Confirmation in Relation to Baptism*. One of the statements of Dix which caused deep concern in the Church of England was: "Christian Initiation in the New Testament is described and conceived of solely in terms of a *conscious* adherence and response to the Gospel of God, that is, solely in terms of an *adult* Initiation." [1] However, Dix seems to modify his statement to a certain extent by saying further that the church may well afford infant baptism provided it is never thought of as normal but always as abnormality.[2] In 1948 Oscar Cullmann, a colleague of Barth at the University of Basle, replied to the pamphlet of Barth with his *Le Baptême des Enfants et la doctrine biblique du baptême*. This took refuge in the analogy of proselyte baptism to justify infant baptism. Joachim Jeremias, followed the same line of argument.[3] The following are among the many recent authors of studies on the subject: W. F. Flemington, J. E. L. Oulton, Marcus Barth, Johannes Schneider, T. W. Manson, and E. A. Payne. Joseph H. Crehan, S. J., has presented the Roman Catholic position.

If there are those in other communions who are honest enough to face the New Testament teaching of baptism in

[1] Dom Gregory Dix, *The Theology of Confirmation in Relation to Baptism* (New York: Morehouse Publishing Co., 1946), p. 31.
[2] *Ibid.*
[3] J. Jeremias, *Hat die älteste Christenheit die Kindertaufe geübt?* (Göttingen: Vandenhoeck und Ruprecht, 1949), pp. 24 ff.

order to see if the teaching of their churches corresponds to that of the New Testament, Baptists ought to be willing to do the same thing since they have maintained throughout the years that they are strictly guided by the New Testament in all matters. Instead of approaching the New Testament to defend the Baptist position, it is necessary to discover what the New Testament presents. Too many theologians and pastors are more bound to the maxims of their communions than they are to the maxims of Christ.

The Meaning of Baptism

Among many Christian groups baptismal practice is in confusion because baptismal theology is so indefinite or, in some cases, faulty. In practice Baptists have been true to the teachings of the New Testament. They have championed immersion as the mode and the believer as the subject. Very little emphasis has been placed, however, on the meaning of baptism for those who submit to it. There is great need for a more thorough study of the biblical evidence which must form the foundation for a more adequate theology of this Christian rite.

No attempt will be made here to treat the possible origins of the Johannine rite of baptism, Jesus' own baptism and its relationship to the meaning of the Johannine rite, the problems connected with Jesus' command to his disciples to baptize (Matt. 28:19 f.), the problems in Acts concerning the relation of baptism to the Holy Spirit, and the relationship between John's baptism and Christian baptism. It will be said only that John's rite looked forward to an event in history that was to come. He called for repentance and baptism in anticipation of the new era. Christian baptism was a proclamation that the new era had arrived. Christians are baptized in the name of the One who has come and not in the name of the One who is to come. While some baptismal theology may be derived from a discussion of the above topics, these topics are more beneficial for arriving at a statement of the practice of baptism in the early church.

For many the sole *raison d'être* of baptism hinges on the command of Jesus to baptize. Baptism is nothing more than following out a demand of Jesus without any awareness of the meaning of the act performed. Is mere obedience to a command all that is involved in baptism? The command to baptize is pointedly coupled with the command to teach those who become disciples. In Matthew 28:19 the two participles of *baptizing* and *teaching* are related to the imperative, *make disciples*. The action of the two participles in relation to the principle verb "make disciples" may be either antecedent to, simultaneous with, or subsequent to. It is more probable that the action is simultaneous. Since the two participles sustain the same relationship to the verb, it would seem that ethical instruction is simultaneous with baptism. The ethical teachings of Jesus, in any case, are vitally related to the act of baptism in the command to baptize in Matthew 28:19 f. To be sure, Christians ought to be obedient to the command of Jesus to baptize, but all other commands have equal claims.

In the study of baptism it is necessary to guard against two extreme positions. The importance of baptism must not be magnified beyond a point warranted by New Testament teaching, and equal care must be given not to minimize the importance of the rite to the extent that it becomes a symbol stripped of all meaning.

The Meaning of Baptism According to Paul

In the book of Acts Christian baptism appears as a practice, while in Paul's epistles and the general epistles baptism is filled with theological content. Paul made no attempt to explain the origin of baptism as he did the Lord's Supper. He acknowledged the rite and did not present the doctrine in a systematic way because he wrote to Christians who were supposed to be familiar with its essential meaning. The contexts in which baptism was mentioned by Paul are, for the most part, passages in which Paul was challenging his readers to a higher type of Christian living.

Magical or symbolical.—It is quite evident that at a very early date Christianity became sacramentarian. Did this departure from the thought of the primitive church begin with the apostle Paul? If sacramentalism had been a Pauline innovation, the apostle surely would have presented this position more clearly and emphatically. There is no evidence that he changed Christianity into a mystery religion and transformed the primitive rites into magical sacraments.

The Pauline doctrine of faith is ample proof that there was no acceptance of ritual as the means of cleansing from sin or of obtaining any benefits associated with salvation. The theme of Romans is a right relationship with God by faith in Jesus Christ. This theme is stated at the very beginning of the epistle and is continued with chief emphasis until the chapter in which the reference to baptism is found (cf. 1:17; 3:22–30; 4:5; 5:1). Had Paul introduced baptism as a magical, efficacious rite, his whole argument for a right relationship with God by faith would have been for nothing.

First Corinthians 10:1–14 alludes to Christian baptism and the Lord's Supper, warning the Christians in Corinth by a parallel drawn from Hebrew history that "no sacramental act achieves anything unless it is an outward symbol of what really happens inwardly in experience." [4] In this passage Paul

[4] C. H. Dodd, *The Meaning of Paul for To-Day* (London: The Swarthmore Press Limited, 1937), p. 119.

looked on the events of the beginning of Israel's history as analogous to the experiences connected with Christian baptism. The Israelites were baptized "into" Moses as the Christians were baptized into Christ. The Christians constituted the new Israel of God, and there is an analogy to the old Israel of God. As the old Israel could not depend on this baptism into Moses for a right relationship with God but must have a new life which was demonstrated by ethical consequences, so it would be impossible for the Christian to depend on the sacraments as security for a right relationship.

It is clear from the passage that the Corinthians were viewing the rite in some way as magical and efficacious, but the warning of Paul was that sacraments in themselves do not avail unless there is obedience to faith.

Union with Christ.—What was the significance of Christian baptism for Paul? The prevailing thought for him seems to be that of a union with Christ, but he also set forth the rite as a symbol of unity in the Christian fellowship. The most characteristic expression used by the apostle to describe the nature of the Christian life is *in Christ*. Deissmann has pointed out that Paul used this phrase and cognate expressions no less than 164 times in his epistles.[5] Some scholars hold that the basis for the doctrine of the mystical union with Christ was based on Paul's experience with Christ and that he has created the expression *in Christ* to portray that experience. It appears that Paul found the formula *in Christ* in primitive Christian use, but the real force and full implications of the formula escaped the minds of the others while Paul was fully aware of them.

It is also possible, as Loisy suggested,[6] that the *in Christ*

[5] A. Deissmann, *Die neutestamentliche Formel 'in Christo Jesu'* (Marburg: n. g. Elwert'sche Verlagsbuchhandlung, 1892), p. 12.

[6] A. Loisy, *Les Mystères Paiens et Le Mystère Chrétien* (2nd ed., Paris, 1921), p. 270, n. 2.

phrases may be shortened forms of the baptismal formula found in Acts. In the book of Acts the expression "in the name of Jesus Christ," or "in the name of the Lord Jesus," is connected with baptism.

The testimony of the papyri indicates that in the Greco-Roman world a name generally stood for the person who bore it. There was some sort of mysterious virtue assigned to the names of the divine beings so that whoever invoked the name of the god was by that invocation brought into a certain relationship with the god. Heitmüller and others[7] hold that the phrase "into the name of Jesus" was charged with superstitious ideas from the pagan world. The pagans believed that if one pronounced the name of a god, the power of that god became his own power.

There seems to be nothing in common with this pagan notion and the formula used for Christian baptism. However, there is a meaning to the invocation of a name that is shared in Semitic and Hellenistic thought. When the name of a person is pronounced over someone, then that person becomes the property of the one whose name is pronounced. When the name of Jesus was invoked in the case of those who were baptized, then the new convert became the possession of Christ. Christ was the owner, and the individual became the servant. If the *in Christ* phrase has any relationship to the formula "into the name of the Lord Jesus," then it would seem that the meaning would be a master-servant relationship, which, to be sure, was one of the favorite themes of the apostle Paul.

From three passages in Paul's epistles the *in Christ* relationship is set forth as a relationship that is properly connected

[7] W. Heitmüller, *Im Namen Jesu* (Göttingen: Vandenhoeck und Ruprecht, 1903), pp. 266–335; Johannes Weiss, *The History of Primitive Christianity*, trans. S. E. Johnson (New York: Wilson-Erickson, 1937), II, 643 ff.

with baptism. The classical source for information about Paul's teaching on baptism and its relationship to Christ is found in Romans 6:1–14. This passage can be understood only in the light of the argument of which it is a part. The theme of the epistle, as has already been stated, is a right relationship with God by faith in Christ. In chapter 4, Paul proved to his Jewish readers that a right relationship does not exist through law, for if they would go back far enough in their review of the teaching of the law, they would discover that Abraham's right relationship with God was on the basis of faith (Rom. 4:1 ff.). Chapter 5, after showing the central position of faith for a right relationship with God, tells of the access of sin through Adam and the consequent dominion of sin. This is followed by the truth that the faith bringing access to God is faith in Christ.

Paul substantiated his claim that salvation does not come by human achievement of righteousness in obedience to a code of precepts but solely by faith. He showed how the universal dominion of sin had issued in good, in that it has revealed the great redemption of God and had given the reign of grace. He reached the climax of this line of thought by stating, "But where sin abounded, grace did much more abound" (Rom. 5:20). Paul realized that this statement would be open to misunderstanding. He had already indicated as much in Romans 3:7–8 but dismissed the thought for clarification at a later place in the epistle. This clarification begins with the sixth chapter, first answering a false conclusion that some might draw from Romans 5:20 by asking the question, "What shall we say then? Shall we continue in sin, that grace may abound?" If grace is so essential, the natural conclusion that one would make is that one should go on sinning to get more grace. Paul was afraid that his readers might take a careless attitude toward sin and become libertines.

Paul's method for meeting such a justification for lax living was to penetrate more radically into the nature of the Christian experience itself and to point out how unreasonable it was to think that anyone who had saving faith could continue in sin. He began from a consideration of baptism and showed how baptism, by its very symbolism, condemns such an idea (Rom. 6:1-14). The discussion of Christian experience is further elaborated, reaching its conclusion in Paul's presentation of the new life in Christ as controlled by the indwelling Spirit of God (Rom. 8:1-13).

Baptism in Romans 6 means the re-enactment of what happened to Christ. Being plunged into the water, the believer demonstrates a dying and burial with Christ; he emerges and is raised with Christ. This connection of death with baptism came from the statement of Jesus in Mark 10:38-39 and Luke 12:50, in which baptism was treated by Jesus as a metaphor referring to his death. Paul used the great events of the Passion to explain the transformation of his own life and the lives of others, which had been accomplished through union with Christ by faith. In Christ's name the believer is plunged beneath the baptismal waters and passes out of contact with the old environment. As he comes up he enters a new environment which is the realm of the Spirit. Faith receives the baptism as the believer's sign of grace manifested in Christ. The Christian believes in the efficacy of baptism not because he believes in the efficacy of the rite but because he believes in the reality—symbolized by the rite—of that which God has manifested in Christ.

Baptism, then, does not become the instrument of salvation, but faith leads to baptism. Baptism is not relative to salvation, but it is relative to recognition of the fact that God gave himself. In baptism the believer participates in the work of Christ. He receives the benefits of a victory which has been achieved by another. In the act he reproduces the history of Christ. It is not by imitation that he makes this reproduction but by identification in his will. One does not become triumphant himself merely by participating in the triumph. He becomes triumphant only as his own life relives that which Christ did. He must submit fully to the will of God as Christ submitted fully to the will of God. Jesus was sent of God and accepted his life and death as fused into service for God and humanity (Mark 10:45; 14:22; Matt. 20:28; 26:28; 1 Cor. 11:24; Luke 22:19–20; John 12:20–30). Baptism becomes a sign and the moment of realization, both internal and personal, of that which is given in Christ. It expresses and makes real God's intention that the believer participate in what has been accomplished in his Son. It intervenes to mark that participation. To be sure, it refers to an objective reality, but it aims also at a subjective reality.

The apostle Paul was faced with a great problem when he proclaimed that a person could come into Christ by faith alone and did not have to become a son of the commandment to follow the Mosaic law. How was he going to keep the Gentile converts from returning to their former way of life? The Jewish Christians could use the law of Moses as a guiding force to hold the converts to the highest level of ethical living. Paul used baptism as a reminder of the high calling which one has in Christ. He showed that baptism represents the beginning of a new life in which there is union with Christ, making the believer know that his old life is dead with Christ. Baptism thus shows the Christian's liberation from the old sphere in the flesh as he enters into the sphere of Christ. The baptized person is called upon to take up an attitude of life agreeable to the inward meaning of baptism. The supreme test of the reality of this new life by union with Christ in baptism is its ethical consequences. If baptism is a death and resurrection for the believer, then a profound revolution has taken place in his life which is demonstrated by a new moral character.

Baptism and ethics.—The interpretation of Romans 6 turns on the word *sumphutoi*, which means "united by growth." The Christian is to be detached from that which dominated him before. Moral slackness and sin are ruled out. Christ becomes for the believer the source of a new moral and spiritual energy. The ethical implications of dying and rising with Christ indicate that the rite had ethical significance for the baptized and "that the Christian at baptism had been made aware of the moral nature of the new life upon which he was entering." [8]

Certain scholars in recent years have observed that in the early church, as in Judaism, baptism was an important occasion for ethical teaching. Certain ethical sections in Paul's epistles (Col. 3:8 to 4:12; Eph. 4:20 to 6:19; Rom. 12:1 f.) and the general epistles (1 Peter; James 1:1 to 4:10; Heb. 12:1 f.) suggest that New Testament writers used certain baptismal, catechetical materials in their role as teachers.

In the Epistle to the Galatians the apostle Paul, in counteracting the Judaizing influence among the Galatian churches, emphasized, as he did in Romans, that the right relationship which Abraham had with God was on the basis of faith and not on the basis of the works of the law (Gal. 3:6 ff.). He told the Galatians that before their faith in Christ was realized they had been kept under lock and key by the law (Gal. 3: 23–24), but now that faith had come, the old *pedagogue* system had terminated for them (Gal. 3:25). "For as many of you as have been baptized into Christ have put on Christ" (3:27). Instead of the metaphor of death and resurrection the

[8] W. D. Davies, *Paul and Rabbinic Judaism* (London: S.P.C.K., 1948), p. 122.

metaphor of clothing is used. Does this figure of speech have any kinship with similar use in the mystery cults? A parallel could hardly be drawn between this idea of Paul and the priestly donning of the divine mask or of Lucius' putting on the twelve robes to dress as the sun. It is also doubtful that the metaphor has any relationship to a baptismal robe. Knox [9] has submitted evidence which would lead one to believe that the figure of speech could be drawn from Judaism. The comparison of a new life to a fresh garment belongs to the Jewish mind as well as to Hellenistic thought. The Old Testament speaks of clothing one with strength, righteousness, glory, salvation, and so on (Prov. 31:25; Job 8:22; 29:14; 39:19; Psalm 93:1; Isa. 51:9; 52:1; 59:17; 61:10; Zech. 3:4; et al.). Paul used similar expressions (Rom. 13:12; 1 Cor. 15:53–54; Eph. 6:11, 14; Col. 3:12; 1 Thess. 5:8). Burton [10] has stated that these passages in Paul's epistles show that the idiom conveyed no suggestion of putting on a mask but referred to an act by which one entered an actual relationship.

The verb that means "to put on" in Galatians 3:27 is endunō. When used with a personal object, this word means "to take on the character or standing" of the person referred to. It denotes that the wearer becomes in a way identified with what he puts on. When a man is baptized into Christ, he becomes so thoroughly identified with him that it is no longer he who lives but it is Christ who lives in him. An expression that was popular among the French at one time was l'habit fait le moine, "the dress makes the monk." When one clothes himself at baptism with Christ he changes his appearance. He is a new creation (Gal. 6:15; 2 Cor. 5:17). The life of Christ

[9] W. L. Knox, St. Paul and the Church of the Gentiles (Cambridge: The University Press, 1939), p. 38.

[10] E. D. Burton, Critical and Exegetical Commentary on the Epistle to the Galatians ("International Critical Commentary" New York: Charles Scribner's Sons, 1920), p. 204.

is manifested in him (2 Cor. 4:17; Eph. 4:24; Gal. 2:19; 6:14–15). It is interesting to note that in Colossians 3:5–17, which is in a baptismal context, the apostle Paul used the figure of clothing. He pointed out that certain things are to be put off and certain things are to be put on. Christians are to put off the old clothes of the old life and put on the new clothes of the new life, which new clothes correspond to the character of Christ.

In Colossians Paul went on to say that in Christ, "also you were circumcised with a circumcision made without hands, by putting off the body of the flesh in the circumcision of Christ" (Col. 2:11, RSV). He described what is meant by Christ's circumcision by saying, "you were buried with him in baptism, in which you were also raised with him through faith in the working of God, who raised him from the dead" (v. 12, RSV).

It seems strange that Paul, in view of the controversies he had encountered over the rite of circumcision, would emphasize a meaning of baptism that could be compared to circumcision. Some relationship here between circumcision and baptism is so obvious that it cannot be denied. However, it is impossible to maintain that baptism takes the place of circumcision and that circumcision under the old age is the same as baptism under the new age. Cullmann sees such a relationship and uses this as one of his chief arguments for infant baptism. Circumcision in this passage seems rather to point to spiritual circumcision and is not anything more than the Pauline view "that union with Christ does away with the necessity for circumcision, and is therefore our initiation into the covenant of Christ." [11] Some scholars contend that the section on baptism in Romans 6 is an expansion of a single verse in Colossians

[11] H. H. Rowley, "The Origin and Meaning of Baptism," *The Baptist Quarterly* (London: The Carey Kingsgate Press, Ltd., 1942–45), XI, 313.

(2:11). Since it is quite possible that Colossians was written from Ephesus rather than from Rome, it may be that Paul expanded the thought in Colossians 2:11 and also repeated some of the material in Colossians 2:20 to 3:17. As in Romans, so here Paul has related baptism to the death and resurrection of Christ. He also pointed out that the circumcision of real value is spiritual (Rom. 4:11) and showed that baptism has ethical consequences (Col. 3:5–17).

In the contrast between spiritual and physical circumcision Paul explained that the putting off of the body of flesh in physical circumcision does not elevate one above the law of sin and death, as described in Romans 7:7–25. Faith in Christ and union with him, which union is depicted in baptism, gives to one the law of the spirit of life which overcomes the law of sin and death. Believers are then in the realm of the Holy Spirit.

In the contrast between physical circumcision and spiritual circumcision (Col. 2:11 f.) one is reminded of the contrast between external removal of dirt from the body in baptism and the internal pledging of human faith to do God's will, (1 Pet. 3:21). In this passage the author put forward his view of that which is distinctive about Christian baptism in both a negative and positive manner by two appositional phrases. Negatively stated, baptism is not the "putting away of the filth of the flesh." The removal of dirt or ceremonial uncleanness is not the meaning of Christian baptism. Peter rejected a ritual purifying with a mere physical or material blamelessness as the aim. The statement seems to be a polemic against a faulty theory of the rite of baptism. Possibly the author intended to contrast the spiritually effective Christian baptism with Judaistic ceremonial cleansings, or perhaps the contrast is with a pagan idea of the observance of the rite.

Positively stated, baptism is "an answer of a good conscience toward God." Reicke,[12] in his masterful exegetical treatment of 1 Peter 3:19 ff., has sought to overcome the difficulty involved in the interpretation of this positive phrase by a study of the words contained in it. The meaning that he discovered for the word translated "conscience" is that of a good or loyal attitude of mind. It is the willingness to fulfil loyally the whole of God's will. Concerning *eperōtēma* (answer), which has been translated as "prayer," "pledge," and "question," Reicke has suggested that the author was "thinking of a special act in the ritual of Baptism, perhaps a statement of belief or something similar, or else . . . an agreement or an undertaking only in a general meaning." [13] Accepting the latter meaning, Reicke has argued that baptism is defined as an undertaking with an ethical meaning that implies an acceptance of the divine demand of a positive habit of mind in loyalty to God. Faith, though not specifically mentioned in this connection, is that which makes the rite efficacious, because in 1 Peter 1:5 faith is shown to be the principle of salvation and in 1:9 salvation is described as the end of faith.

Union with believers.—While his predominant idea of baptism is union with Christ, Paul also suggested that baptism is a symbol of the unity of believers in Christ. The apostle was deeply concerned for the existence of unity in the Christian fellowship. He was so much concerned for friendly relations between Jewish Christians and Gentile Christians that he encouraged the Gentile churches to take up an offering and send it to the poor saints in Jerusalem in order to cement peaceful relations between the two. The plan failed, and Paul was worse off for it. He consistently maintained, how-

[12] Bo Ivar Reicke, *The Disobedient Spirits and Christian Baptism* (Kobenhavn: E. Munksgaard, 1946), pp. 173–207.
[13] Reicke, *op. cit.*, p. 185.

ever, that in Christ all racial and social differences were erased and as a result there was one new humanity. All Christians were in the realm of the Holy Spirit, and traditional distinctions were obliterated. There is sufficient basis for the Pauline appeal because Peter on the day of Pentecost, in explaining the ecstatic action of the disciples, exclaimed, "This is that which was spoken by the prophet Joel" (Acts 2:16). Peter quoted the prophetic utterance of Joel which emphasized the democratizing of the Holy Spirit, and he defined the new age set forth by Joel as his own time. The predicted time had arrived in Christ who sent his Spirit upon all flesh. No distinctions were to be made.

The special note of Paul in his Ephesian letter is that the church is the body of Christ. This idea is advanced in Colossians 1:18, but the expansion of this thought is in Ephesians 1:22 ff. As Christ was incarnate historically, so now he is incarnate spiritually in his church, which is his body. In Christ all humanity becomes one. Christ broke down the middle wall of partition that separated Jew from Gentile and reconciled both unto God in one body by the cross (Eph. 2:11 ff.) Ephesians 4:5 mentions baptism as one of the marks of the unity of the Christian fellowship.

In the church at Corinth various members prided themselves upon their gifts, and each felt that his gift excelled those of the other Christians. In trying to point out the importance of all gifts, Paul used the body and its members as a figure of speech. This "body" is connected with baptism and the Spirit. "For by one Spirit we are all baptized into one body —Jews or Greeks, slaves or free—and all were made to drink of one Spirit" (1 Cor. 12:13, RSV). Here baptism is viewed as the rite which the Spirit uses for binding men into the unity of the Christian fellowship. Baptism becomes the bond of union of believers. It is "the 'effective symbol' whereby all

Christians are made one in Christ and racial and social distinctions transcended." [14]

Following the statement, "For as many of you as were baptized into Christ have put on Christ" (Gal. 3:27, RSV), the apostle wrote, "There is neither Jew nor Greek, there is neither slave nor free, there is neither male nor female; for you are all one in Christ Jesus." By becoming a Christian, a Gentile can be considered the posterity of Abraham, since those who have been baptized have been clothed with the character of Christ. This identification with Christ has effaced all distinctions. The same idea is advanced in Colossians 3:9 ff. Since baptism is a symbol of unity in the Christian fellowship, whatever distinctions exist in the body of believers make baptism an ineffective symbol of the Christian faith. The validity of such baptism is open to question.

Baptism is a symbol of union with Christ. The Christian's life is essentially a spiritual union with Christ through personal commitment and trust. In being united with Christ the believer submits to the perfect will of God, even as Christ submitted to it. This is a union that does not tend toward sacramentalism. When the individual is united with Christ in baptism, he also becomes incorporated into a spiritual society, the church, which is the body of Christ. Being incorporated into this spiritual society removes all distinctions between Christians and creates oneness in Christ. Understanding baptism as union with Christ and with all believers, carrying the highest ethical meaning, is an important step toward keeping the new commandment of Jesus, that Christians love one another.

[14] W. F. Flemington, *The New Testament Doctrine of Baptism* (London: S.P.C.K., 1948), p. 57.

V

THE NEW TESTAMENT SIGNIFICANCE OF THE LORD'S SUPPER

Dale Moody

O NE OF THE SIGNS of return to the New Testament view of the church is the revival of interest in the meaning of the Lord's Supper. This central act of worship is no mere form in New Testament faith. It is freighted with meaning that lifts worship out of empty futility into vital faith in the Son of God who gave himself for us. What the Passover was to the Old Covenant the Lord's Supper is to the New.[1] The significance of the Lord's Supper in the New Testament, organized around the words of institution, points to the present, past, and future.

The Present Significance

The present significance of the Lord's Supper is indicated by the two Greek words so often evident, *eucharistia* and *koinōnia*. The first word signifies the Lord's Supper as thanksgiving, and the second word signifies the Lord's Supper as participation.

---

[1] This statement is greatly strengthened by the Passover theory of the origin of the Lord's Supper so profoundly stated in Joachim Jeremias, *The Eucharistic Words of Jesus*, trans. A. Ehrhardt (Oxford: Basil Blackwell, 1955).

79

The Lord's Supper as thanksgiving.—Serious study of the New Testament sources of the Lord's Supper soon notices the emphasis on thanksgiving. Mark 14:22 and Matthew 26:26 say that Jesus gave the bread to the disciples when he had "blessed" (*eulogēsas*) it, and 1 Corinthians 11:24 and Luke 22:19 say this happened "when he had given thanks" (*eucharistēsas*). Mark 14:23 and Matthew 26:27 say that he gave the cup to them after he had given thanks (*eucharistēsas*), while 1 Corinthians 11:25 and Luke 22:20 say the bread and the cup were given in the same manner. It is safe to conclude, then, that no great distinction can be made between *eulogia* and *eucharistia* in the accounts of the Lord's Supper. The loaf and the cup were blessed by the words of thanksgiving spoken over them.

The eucharistic emphasis is not altogether absent from other New Testament references to the Supper. The apostolic practice consisted in devotion to "the apostles' teaching and fellowship, to the breaking of bread and the prayers" (Acts 2:42). Besides "attending the temple together and breaking bread in their homes, they partook of food with glad and generous hearts, praising God and having favor with all the people" (Acts 2:46–47, RSV). Paul commanded the Christians of Corinth to clean out the leaven of sin in order to celebrate the sacrifice of Christ, the paschal Lamb (1 Cor. 5:7 f.). This idea of celebration and blessing centers in "the cup of blessing which we bless," but it is not altogether absent from the loaf (1 Cor. 10:16). It is difficult to resist the conclusion that John saw eucharistic significance in the feeding of the five thousand when he recalled how Jesus gave thanks (*eucharistēsas*) over the loaves (John 6:11, 23). Mark 8:6 also uses *eucharistēsas*, and *eulogēsen* is used in Mark 6:41.

Just what words of thanksgiving were spoken is not certain, but some idea can be gained from the *Berakoth* in the

Mishnah, the *Didache,* and the *First Apology* of Justin. The blessing over the bread in Jewish usage was: "Praised be thou, O Lord our God, King of the Universe, who bringest forth bread from the earth." [2] The blessing over the cup was: "Praised be thou, O Lord our God, King of the Universe, who creates the fruit of the vine." [3] The *Didache* instructs the readers to celebrate the Eucharist by giving thanks over both the cup and the broken bread. The words over the cup are: "We thank Thee, our Father, for the holy Vine of David Thy Servant, which Thou didst make known to us through Jesus Thy Servant; to Thee be the glory for ever." [4] The words over the bread were: "We thank Thee, our Father, for the life and knowledge which Thou didst make known to us through Jesus Thy Servant; to Thee be the glory for ever. Even as this bread that is broken was scattered upon the mountains and being gathered together was made one, so let Thy Church be gathered together from the ends of the earth into Thy kingdom, for Thine is the glory and the power through Jesus Christ for ever." [5] Justin described the Eucharist in some detail with echoes of previous practice as follows:

There is then brought to the president of the brethren bread and a cup of wine mixed with water; and he taking them, gives praise and glory to the Father of the universe, Through the name of the Son and of the Holy Ghost, and offers thanks at considerable length for our being counted worthy to receive these things at His hands. And when he had concluded the prayers and thanksgivings all the people present express assent by saying Amen. [6]

[2] *Berakoth* 6:1.
[3] *Ibid.*
[4] *Didache* 9:2.
[5] *Didache* 9:3–4.
[6] Justin Martyr, *First Apology,* LXV.

In the light of these facts it seems certain that early Christianity celebrated the Lord's Supper as a thanksgiving (*eucharistia*).[7]

The Lord's Supper as participation.—The participation of the disciples in the body and blood of the Lord is suggested in the liturgical commands in the accounts of institution. This emphasis is especially clear in Matthew, as can be seen in a comparison of Matthew 26:26–27 with Mark 14:22–23. The meaning suggested by the words of institution are clearly elaborated in apostolic practice.

After his death and resurrection, Jesus appeared to his disciples in community meals (Luke 24:30–35, 36–43; John 21:9–14; Acts 1:4; 10:41). This is apparently the origin of "the breaking of the bread," which is so distinctive in Luke-Acts (Luke 24:30, 35; Acts 2:42, 26; 20:7, 11; 27:35). Both the spiritual and social significance of "the breaking of the bread" are evident in the life of the Jerusalem church. Immediately following the statement of their devotion "to the apostles' teaching and fellowship, to the breaking of the bread and the prayers" is the first famous passage on the community of goods. Acts 2:44–46 says:

And all who believed were together and had all things in common; and they sold their possessions and goods and distributed them to all, as any had need. And day by day, attending the temple together and breaking bread in their homes, they partook of food with glad and generous hearts (RSV).

Paul arrived in Troas five days "after the days of Unleavened Bread" and celebrated the breaking of bread at the end of seven days "on the first day of the week" (Acts 20:6 f.).

[7] *Ibid.*, LXVI. For detailed references to the eucharistic element see Frank Gavin, *The Jewish Antecedents of the Christian Sacraments* (London: S.P.C.K., 1928, 1933).

This would mean that "the days of Unleavened Bread" ended on Tuesday, Paul arrived in Troas on "the first day of the week" and on the following "first day" gathered with the Christians to "break bread." After the incident with Eutychus, Paul broke bread and ate, almost certain evidence that he celebrated the Lord's Supper with them (Acts 20:11).

The silence about the wine in "the breaking of the bread" has led many, notably Hans Lietzmann, to distinguish two types of Eucharist, one of which had no reference to the death of Jesus and the other following Paul in making the death of Christ central.[8] This theory makes much of the shorter text in Luke 22:15–19, contending that Luke gives further evidence of the absence of the eucharistic cup. It seems, however, impossible to make such a radical distinction. The idea of a joyful *agapē* (love feast), as mentioned in Jude 12, is not absent from Paul (cf. 1 Cor. 11:26; 16:22). In fact, the meal was a bit too joyful in Corinth, and this perhaps led Paul to emphasize the death of Christ in contrast to Corinthian excesses (1 Cor. 11:17–22). Paul's emphasis on "the body and the blood of the Lord" (1 Cor. 11:27) was a corrective for the ethical sophistications in the church in Corinth.

Three examples illuminate the communion (*koinōnia*) of the Lord's Supper.

First, Paul wrote in 1 Corinthians 5 of a case of incest. This arrogant defiance of Christian moral standards drove him to pronounce "judgment in the name of the Lord Jesus" on the guilty man (vv. 3–4, RSV) and to instruct the church to "deliver this man to Satan for the destruction of the flesh, that his spirit may be saved in the day of the Lord Jesus" (v. 5). The apostle was writing at about the time of the Pass-

[8] A. J. B. Higgins, *The Lord's Supper in the New Testament* (London: S.C.M. Press, 1952), pp. 56–63.

over (cf. 16:8), suggesting the background for a parable drawn from the effect of leaven in a lump:

> Your boasting is not good. Do you not know that a little leaven ferments the whole lump of dough? . . . As you really are unleavened. For Christ, our paschal lamb, has been sacrificed. Let us, therefore, celebrate the festival, not with the old leaven, the leaven of malice and evil, but with the unleavened bread of sincerity and truth (5:6–8, RSV).

It is clear that excommunication was vitally related to the *koinōnia* of the Lord's Supper when Paul explained that his former letter did not relate to the immoral who were outside the church but meant they were "not to associate with any one who bears the name of brother if he is guilty of immorality or greed, or is an idolator, reviler, drunkard, or robber—not even to eat with such a one" (v. 11). This eating "with such a one" is almost surely a reference to the Lord's Supper.

The second example relates to eating meat that had been offered to idols (1 Cor. 10:16–21). God was displeased with the fathers even after they "were baptized into Moses in the cloud and in the sea," even those who ate the supernatural food (Ex. 16:4, 35) and drank the supernatural drink (Ex. 17:16; Num. 10:11). Paul saw in this a warning for the instruction of those "upon whom the end of the ages has come" (1 Cor. 10:1–5, 11). So the Corinthians should not presume upon God even if they possessed knowledge and had been baptized into the body of Christ. Their attitude toward the weaker brethren could destroy the *koinōnia* of the body of Christ and lead them into the impossible situation in which they would try to be partners in the table of demons. This distinction between "the table of the Lord and the table of demons" (1 Cor. 10:21) is one of the major points in

the understanding of the *koinōnia* of the Lord's Supper.[9]
How can one read 1 Corinthians 10:16–21, so loaded with
the idea of communion *koinōnia*, and deny that Paul thought
of the Lord's Supper as a communion meal?

The cup of blessing [*eulogias*] which we bless [*eulogoumen*],
is it not a participation [*koinōnia*] in the blood of Christ? The
bread [loaf] which we break, is it not a participation [*koinōnia*]
in the body of Christ? Because there is one loaf, we who are
many are one body, for we all partake [*metechomen*] of the
same loaf. Consider the practice of Israel; are not those who eat
the sacrifices partners [*koinōnoi*] in the altar? What do I imply
then? That food offered to idols is anything, or that an idol is
anything? No, I imply that what pagans sacrifice they offer to
demons and not to God. I do not want you to be partners
[*konōnous*] with demons. . . . You cannot partake [*metechein*]
of the table of the Lord and the table of demons (RSV).

It will be noticed that the Greek words *metochē* and *koinōnia*,
like the words *eulogia* and *eucharistia*, have no major difference in meaning. The most that can be said is that *metochē*
is used to describe the partaking of food. It is possible, but
not certain, that the significance of the one loaf formed the
basis for thinking of the church as the one body of Christ.[10]

The third example concerns public worship (1 Cor. 11:
17–34). The divisions arising out of class distinctions destroyed the *koinōnia* of the church (vv. 23–26). How could
the Lord's Supper be celebrated in a worthy manner after
an *agapē* (love feast) that left the marks of class distinction
and social cleavage? Such action disgraced the church and
humiliated the poor. The social implications of this account
are too obvious for contemporary comfort, but the emphasis
on *koinōnia* (fellowship) at the Lord's Supper rescues the

[9] L. S. Thornton, *The Common Life in the Body of Christ* (Westminster: The Dacre Press, 1942), pp. 322 ff.
[10] *Ibid.*, p. 330.

ordinance from the unimportance to which many relegate it. The tradition (*paradosis*) which Paul received from the Lord is next related (vv. 23–26).

The concept of discerning the body of the Lord (vv. 27–32) has given rise to the various traditional theories of Christ's presence in the bread and wine. One view argues that discerning the body of the Lord means accepting the dogma of transubstantiation, in which the elements of the bread and wine are looked upon as the actual body and blood of the Lord. This interpretation has been rejected by those supporting the spiritual interpretation, which understands the discernment of the body as insight into the *koinōnia* of the church proclaimed by the ordinance. All that has been said thus far supports the spiritual interpretation. In fact, a deep division in Christian *koinōnia* (fellowship) took place when much of the church ceased discerning the spiritual significance of the risen body of Christ and professed to devour the substance of the earthly body of Christ.

The *Didache* indicates that baptism (9:5) and confession of sin (14:1) must precede the celebration of the Lord's Supper (cf. 1 Cor. 10:1–4). The dialogue in *Didache* 10:6 is a dramatic description of the liturgy:

The Leader: Let grace come and let this world pass away!

The Congregation: Hosanna to the Son of David!

The Leader: If any man be holy, let him come, if any man be not, let him repent! *Maranatha.*

The Congregation: Amen. [11]

Perhaps the "holy kiss" [12] was a custom in connection with this liturgy.

[11] Oscar Cullmann, *Early Christian Worship*, trans. A. Stewart Todd and James B. Torrance (London: SCM Press Ltd., 1953), pp. 19 f.
[12] 1 Cor. 16:20; 2 Cor. 13:12; 1 Thess. 5:26; Rom. 16:16; 1 Pet. 5:14.

Controversy over close communion usually centers on the validity of baptism, which all agree precedes the Lord's Supper, but the question of confession of sin and congregational discipline too often drops into the background. It takes far more than membership in a local church holding correct doctrine to qualify for participation in the Lord's Supper. The moral issues were deeply significant in the New Testament churches.[13]

The Past Significance

The Lord's Supper is not only a sign of the present reality of *eucharistia* and *koinōnia* but also serves to recall certain past events in the Christian faith. These are the ideas of a covenant (*diathēkē*) and a recollection (*anamnēsis*).

The Lord's Supper as covenant.—The heart of the Pentateuch is the story of the Lord's deliverance of Israel from Egyptian bondage. The mighty act of the Lord, described in Exodus 1–15, was remembered annually through the ages at the celebration of the Passover.[14] The Exodus is the story of the making of the covenant, and the covenant established the normal relation between Israel and the Lord.[15] The covenant, therefore, may be considered the central idea of the Old Testament.[16]

The preparation of the Passover for the Lord's Supper is evident from the mention of the covenant in all four accounts of institution (Mark 14:24; Matt. 26:26; Luke 22:20; 1 Cor. 11:25). Some, indeed, have argued that the reference to the

[13] A classic Baptist statement on this issue is J. L. Dagg, "A Treatise on Church Order," *Manual of Theology* (Charleston: Southern Baptist Publication Society, 1859), pp. 203–225.

[14] Johannes Pedersen, *Israel: Its Life and Culture* (Copenhagen: Paul Branner, 1940), III–IV, 726–737.

[15] *Ibid.*, p. 654.

[16] Walter Eichrodt, *Theologie des Alten Testaments* (Leipzig: J. C. Hinrichs Verlag, 1933), I.

covenant forms "no part of the original tradition of this saying of Jesus." [17] Discussions center on two points. The first has to do with the blood of the covenant. Some Jewish scholars find it "quite impossible to admit that Jesus would have said to his disciples that they should eat of his body and drink of his blood." [18] Yet it seems that two great sacrificial ideas meet in this saying over the cup. The mention of the covenant recalls the sprinkling of dedicated blood at Sinai (Ex. 24:8) when the Israelites "saw God, and did eat and drink" (Ex. 24:11); and the blood of the covenant, represented by the red wine in the cup, defined the atoning significance of the blood of Jesus which would be poured out for many. This adds the idea of the Suffering Servant in Isaiah 53:12, who "poured out his soul to death" and "bore the sin of many." John 6:51–58 is a vivid reminder that the drinking of blood and the eating of flesh was repugnant to the Jews of Jesus' day. Efforts to regard the eucharistic emphasis in John 6:51–58 a redaction have not succeeded, and it must be considered a vital part of the discourse. [19]

The second point of discussion pertains to the idea of the *new* covenant. Both Luke 22:20 and 1 Corinthians 11:25 speak of the covenant as being new. There is textual evidence, of course, that Luke 22:19–20 is an interpolation (presumably from 1 Corinthians 11:24 f.), leaving the idea of the new covenant in Paul only. The passage in Luke is recognized as a difficult textual problem, and advocates of the longer version should be sobered by the fact that the Westcott-Hort text favors the shortest version. Yet it seems to the writer that the strongest evidence is in favor of the

[17] A. J. B. Higgins, *op. cit.*, p. 33.

[18] Joseph Klausner, *Jesus of Nazareth* (New York: The Macmillan Company, 1929), p. 329.

[19] E. C. Hoskyns, *The Fourth Gospel* (London: Faber & Faber, Ltd., 1946), p. 305; Oscar Cullmann, *op. cit.*, pp. 93–105.

longer version.[20] With the support of the longer version in Luke, it seems correct to say that Jesus regarded his death the fulfilment of the new covenant proclaimed by Jeremiah 31: 27–34 (cf. Heb. 8:8–12; 10:16–17). Second Corinthians 3:6 makes it clear that the idea of a new covenant was used by Paul. It is excessive dogmatism to declare that Jesus cannot be the source of the saying both in Luke and Paul.[21]

Tertullian used the word *sacramentum* (sacrament) to describe baptism.[22] The word originally meant a vow made by a soldier, and this meaning is not far from the idea of a covenant. However, Tertullian and many who have used the word to describe baptism and the Lord's Supper have loaded it with ideas that confuse the true meaning of the word. It is better, therefore, to avoid the word when speaking of the Lord's Supper as a new covenant in the blood of Christ. The term "ordinance" is used to avoid the erroneous connotations of "sacramentalism."

The Lord's Supper as recollection.—For a clearer understanding of the Greek word *anamnēsis*, used in the words of institution of the Lord's Supper in Luke 22:19 and 1 Corinthians 11:24–25, it is useful to compare it with the ideas of memory and discernment. The word for memory is *mnēmosunon*. It is used in connection with the Passover in a manner preparatory for the Lord's Supper, but it is not adequate to express the full meaning of the Lord's saving benefits to his own. The following examples in the Old Testament are illuminating: "This day shall be for you a memorial [*lezikkaron*, Septuagint, *mnēmosunon*] day, and you shall keep it as a feast to the Lord; throughout your generations

---

[20] C. S. C. Williams, *Alterations to the Text of the Synoptic Gospels and the Acts* (Oxford: Basil Blackwell, 1951), pp. 47–51, supports the longer version with full discussion.

[21] A. J. B. Higgins, *op. cit.*, pp. 32 f.

[22] *De baptismo* 1–5, 8–9, 11, 13.

you shall observe it as an ordinance for ever" (Ex. 12:14).

"And it shall be to you as a sign on your hand and as a memorial [*lezikkaron*, Septuagint, *mnēmosunon*] between your eyes, that the law of the Lord may be in your mouth; for with a strong hand the Lord has brought you out of Egypt. You shall therefore keep this ordinance at its appointed time from year to year" (Ex. 13:9–10, RSV). Compare Deuteronomy 16:3 and Exodus 13:3.

The word *mnēmosunon* is used in the New Testament in connection with the memorial to the woman in Mark 14:9 who anointed Jesus for burial. It would seem, however, that the word *anamnēsis* is much stronger than the idea of memorial and is best translated "recollection." *Anamnēsis* appears in the Greek Old Testament in sacrificial associations, especially in Leviticus 24:7 and Numbers 10:10, but it is a mistake to say the Lord's Supper is no more than a memorial to the death of Jesus. The sayings, "This is my body" and "This cup is the new covenant in my blood," have both prophetic and priestly significance.[23] The prophetic significance looks toward the actual breaking of the body and spilling of the blood of Jesus. Against the background of parabolic action in prophetism, it is not difficult to see that Jesus was saying, "This means my body," and, "This cup means the new covenant in my blood." A comparison with Mark 4:15–20 is sufficient clarification, but the dramatic actions of Isaiah (8:3; 20:2), Jeremiah (19:10; 28:10), Ezekiel (4:3), and Agabus (Acts 21:11) would indicate the act was "effective representation," not sacramental transubstantiation.[24]

The priestly significance emphasizes the fact that Jesus

[23] Vincent Taylor, *Jesus and His Sacrifice* (London: Macmillan and Company, 1937), pp. 118–125.

[24] Rudolf Otto, *The Kingdom of God and the Son of Man*, trans. Floyd V. Filson and Bertram Lee-Wolf (London: Lutterworth Press, 1943), pp. 302–305.

was no mere prophet, for Jesus looked upon his death as a sacrificial offering for men. Any view of his death that reduces him to a mere martyr is inadequate to express the surrendered life that was given. Dalman thinks the Greek corresponds to the Aramaic *den hu guphi*, which can be taken in the sense, "This is myself," and the act of eating on the part of the disciples indicates the appropriation of the blessings made available by his vicarious death.

The meaning of *anamnēsis* may be made clearer by reference to classical, biblical, and patristic usage. Plato has indicated that the favorite doctrine of Socrates was that knowledge is simply recollection [*anamnēsis*]. One of Socrates' arguments for immortality was built on the belief that knowledge can be recalled from a pre-existent state.[25] In a discussion that distinguishes the conscious and the unconscious, he declared that memory and recollection must be distinguished, defining recollection as the power which the soul has of recovering the experiences of the body.[26] Aristotle also declared that recollection is more than memory, being the power to recall to the conscious from the unconscious, from the potential to the actual.[27] Too much emphasis must not be given to classical usage, but the references indicate that recollection is not necessarily implied in memory but memory is always implied in recollection.

The Septuagint use of *anamnēsis* in Leviticus 24:7 and Numbers 10:10 has already been mentioned. The word describes the memorial bread in the former passage and memorial sacrifice in the latter. The Apocrypha gives an example:

For they had a token of preservation to remind [*eis anamnēsis*] them of the commandment of your law;

[25] Plato, *Phaedo*, 72e, 92d.
[26] Plato, *Philebus*, 34c.
[27] Aristotle, *De memoria et reminiscentia*, 451b.

For the one who turned toward it was saved not because of what
    he saw,
But because of you, who are the preserver of all (Wisd. of Sol.
    16: 6–7, Goodspeed).

The New Testament uses the word without reference to
the Lord's Supper as follows: "But in these sacrifices there is
a reminder [*anamnēsis*] of sin year after year" (Heb. 10:3,
RSV). After the New Testament, Clement of Rome wrote:
"For you have understanding, you have a good understanding of the sacred Scriptures, beloved, and you have studied
the oracles of God. Therefore, we write these things to remind you [*pros anamnēsin*]" (1 Clement 53:3).

Such examples have shown that *anamnēsis* is a powerful
word meaning recalling from one life to another, from the
unconscious to the conscious, and from the past to the present.
So it is not too much to say that the New Testament usage
in connection with the Lord's Supper indicates that a past
event has become a present reality in the act of *anamnēsis*
in Christian worship.

The discernment of this present reality of the body is indicated by the word *diakrinō*. First Corinthians 11:27–32 declares:

Whoever, therefore, eats the bread or drinks the cup of the
Lord in an unworthy manner will be guilty of profaning the
body and blood of the Lord. Let a man examine himself, and so
eat of the bread and drink of the cup. For any one who eats and
drinks without discerning [*diakrinōn*] the body eats and drinks
judgment [*krima*] upon himself. That is why many of you are
weak and ill, and some have died [fallen asleep]. But if we judged
[*diekrinomen*] ourselves truly, we should not be judged
[*ekrinometha*]. But when we are judged [*krinomenoi*] by the
Lord, we are chastened so that we may not be condemned
[*katakrithōmen*] along with the world (RSV).

Paul has distinguished three judgments related to the discernment of the body in the Lord's Supper: self-examination, chastening, and condemnation. Those who practice self-examination are not chastened by the Lord, and those chastened by the Lord are not condemned with the world.

So it may be said that the proper celebration of the Lord's Supper is an act of worship in which the Lord's sacrifice is recalled, not repeated, so that blessing results for those who discern the spiritual significance of the body and chastening results for those who lack discernment.

The Future Significance

The future significance of the Lord's Supper pertains to the kingdom of God—emphasized by Mark, Matthew, and Luke-Acts—and the coming of Christ—emphasized by Paul.

The kingdom of God.—The centrality of the kingdom of God in the teaching of Jesus is denied by none. The reign of the Lord, which has ever been a reality and of which the rulers of Israel were representative, was not established in earth as in heaven until Jesus came. The Old Testament had looked forward in hope that out of the remnant of Israel would come a ruler in whom the sovereign reign of God would become a historical reality. When Jesus appeared, the kingdom of God came in his person and preaching, and those who repent and follow Jesus enter the kingdom (Mark 1:14 f.; Matt. 12:28; 13:16 f.; Luke 19:9, 11; 11:20, 31 f.; 16:16).

Yet there is a future messianic banquet of eschatological joy of which the celebration of the Lord's Supper is a foretaste. This hope transforms Christ's death from the sorrow of parting into the joy of expectation. At the Passover the deliverance from Egypt had proclaimed to Israel a greater redemption to come, and when Jesus spoke of the full realization of the kingdom of God, the thought of a banquet of exceeding joy was ever on his mind (Matt. 8:11; 22:1; Luke 13:29; 22:30). The presentation of this Passover hope at the Lord's Supper is clear in Luke 22:15–18:

And he said to them, "I have earnestly desired to eat this passover with you before I suffer; for I tell you I shall not eat it until it is fulfilled in the kingdom of God." And he took a cup, and when he had given thanks he said, "Take this, and divide it among yourselves; for I tell you that from now on I shall not drink of the fruit of the vine until the kingdom of God comes" (RSV).

The third saying at the Lord's Supper is eschatological (Mark 14:25; Matt. 26:26) and reveals the hope of the kingdom of God beyond the sufferings and death of the cross. Jesus, fully conscious of the imminence of his redemptive sacrifice, anticipated the consummation of history in the kingdom of God. The drinking of the wine at the Supper, being both a participation and a proclamation of that future and more perfect fellowship, rang with the joyful hope that when the kingdom of God would be established, Jesus and his disciples would drink wine at the messianic banquet. This hope goes back to Isaiah 25:6, and its genuineness on the lips of Jesus is beyond question.[28]

Much debate goes on about the relationship between Luke 22:15–18 and Mark 14:25, and the problem may never be solved. Yet, according to the Passover theory, it is possible to assign Luke 22:15–18 to the Passover and Mark 14:25 to the Lord's Supper. Mark 14:25 says: "Truly, I say to you, I shall not drink again of the fruit of the vine until that day when I drink it new in the kingdom of God."

The Lord's Supper was filled with joy in the celebration of the early church because it was an anticipation of the king-

[28] Taylor, *op. cit.*, p. 547.

dom of God. It is this eschatological joy that explains the gladness and generosity which attended "the breaking of bread" (Acts 2:46).

The coming of Christ.—It seems impossible for the writers of the New Testament to think of the kingdom of God apart from the coming of Christ. As far back as Daniel 7 the ideas of the kingdom and of the Messiah are intertwined.

Any effort to show that Paul substituted the sacrificial idea of the Lord's Supper for the eschatological is unable to do justice to the total teaching of Paul. The first letter of Paul to the Corinthians, so rich in sacrificial teachings related to the Lord's Supper, contains some of the great eschatological teachings of the New Testament. Paul gave the opinion that the unmarried should not seek marriage "in view of the impending distress" (1 Cor. 7:26 f.), the fact that "the appointed time has grown very short" (1 Cor. 7:29), and the thought that "the form of this world is passing away" (1 Cor. 7:31). A new Exodus had taken place, and Christians now lived where the ages overlap (1 Cor. 10:1–5, 11), and the resurrection of Jesus after his death was the first fruits of the full harvest (1 Cor. 15:23) when those asleep in death would "be changed, in a moment, in the twinkling of an eye, at the last trumpet" (1 Cor. 15:51–52). In the very narrative of the Lord's Supper, Paul comments on the *paradosis* (tradition) received of the Lord: "For as often as you eat this bread and drink the cup, you proclaim the Lord's death until he comes" (1 Cor. 11:26). The judgment of the Lord awaits the world, so the Lord chastens the members of the church so that they will escape this condemnation (1 Cor. 11:32). Paul was not only sacrificial in his view of the Lord's Supper; he was also eschatological.

It is not enough to state the meaning of the Lord's Supper. Problems raised by critical study should be discussed in detail for the value that may result. Other questions pertaining to denominational and congregational practice must be faced in all fairness and good faith if careful study is to be translated into true piety and devotion. At this point, however, such problems and questions have been left for the time when the significance of the Lord's Supper has been clarified to some degree. The manner of the Lord's Supper is shaped by its meaning.

VI

THE ANABAPTIST VIEW
OF THE CHURCH

Theron D. Price

A FRESH AND FAR-RANGING interest in Anabaptist studies is an encouraging fact of the present. The Anabaptist movement, now more generally and more accurately referred to as the "left wing" of the Reformation, is being widely reassessed and better understood. This is good. There is much in the movement not alone of historical significance but also of perennial relevance. Strong men of simple faith, for example, to whom faithful witness was more important than personal safety, are not to be ignored. To many of these selfless martyrs execution was accepted as a coronation. The vision of God had left nought to fear from men. Far from being merely a species of irresponsible fanaticism (*Schwärmerei*), the left wing in its best representatives shows a fine ethical sensitivity. Witness, for example, the *Schleitheim Articles* or Menno's exposition of the meaning of the cross.

It is good, also, to be reminded that a few left wing emphases, which in the sixteenth century were considered not merely novel but also dangerous, are in the twentieth accepted as axioms by many of the descendants of the left wing's first opponents. It is significant that the substance of recent statements on freedom for believer and for congregation, made by the Executive Committee of the World Council of Churches, could have been written by sixteenth-century

Anabaptists. This emphasis on liberty and on the allied subject of the separation of church and state may now be called the common heritage of American churches.

Because of the recovery of long lost and unedited source materials from the archives of Europe, as well as the possibility of sound generalization on the basis of recent reliable monographs (mainly German), it is now possible to speak with some assurance of the nature of the left wing movement and of its views of the church. The picture which begins to emerge shows clearly that the Anabaptist party (the party of the *restitution* as distinguished from the party of the *reformation*) can no longer be ignored as peripheral or condemned as dangerous.

But more than this begins to appear from the current study. The left wing movement itself was far from uniform. Luther and others lumped people together in a common contumely who would hardly have recognized each other as adherents of the same religion. There was wide diversity among "Anabaptists" in doctrine, in organization, and in the nature of the eschatological hope. To condemn the whole movement under the head of a Münzer-type radicalism, therefore, simply will not do.

The beginnings of the main Anabaptist movement, it is now generally agreed, are traceable not to Wittenburg (Münzer, Karlstadt) or elsewhere but to Zürich and the early Zwingli-circle (Grebel, Manz, Reublin, Blaurock, and, in a lesser sense, Hübmaier). Such is the view of Troeltsch as opposed to Holl. This is also shown in the excellent works by the Mennonite historians at Goshen. It is also clear at last that Anabaptists cannot be neatly accounted for in terms of: (1) succession from radical, brotherhood movements from the Middle Ages, stressing either mysticism and ethical concern (Ludwig Keller) or the visible church and

Christian perfection (Albrecht Ritschl); or (2) economic revolution in religious garb (Karl Kautsky and Belfort Bax). Rather, it is seen that neither the primary evidence on Anabaptist history on the one hand nor the Lutheran and Zwinglian polemic against the Anabaptists on the other can be understood at all until it is recognized that Anabaptism was a distinctive approach to Christianity which threatened *certain aspects* of the Reformation as much as it threatened the Roman Catholic Church. On the Anabaptist principle a community of faith and committed discipleship must emerge in response to the Christian gospel and must demonstrate the quality of divine life within itself. This would require the maintenance of high standards of admittance for those without and the proper exercise of discipline on those within. This is to say that the clue to the Anabaptist interpretation of Christianity is the Anabaptist view of the church.

The truth of this position has been demonstrated from the sources in the recent and splendid volume by Franklin H. Littell.[1] This work, essentially an essay in definition, provides English readers for the first time with a comprehensive analysis of the essence of Anabaptism and its understanding of the church. Since the doctrine of the church increasingly appears to be the crucial category for understanding the left wing generally, it is perhaps not too much to say that Littell's book opens up new possibilities for Reformation research

[1] *The Anabaptist View of the Church, an Introduction to Sectarian Protestantism* ("Studies in Church History," Vol. VIII, Philadelphia: American Society of Church History, 1952). Littell's volume, far more significant than its size would suggest, is the immediate inspiration and provides much of the material for the present article. An appreciative review by T. D. Price may be read in the *Review and Expositor*, Vol. L, No. 1 (Jan., 1953), pp. 90–92.

Effort is made here to communicate as much of this fine work as can easily be done in one short statement. Such exposition and interpretation as appear in the present essay presuppose and rest upon the solid research of Dr. Littell.

along a fairly wide front. The work is also of high importance for what it implies for the current theological revival and for contemporary ecumenical conversation.

The Anabaptist View in Its Original Context and Distinctive Character

Single exceptions to the remarks which follow may not only be suspected on principle but documented by fact. The description which follows must run the dangers attendant upon any synoptic presentation of a historical problem. The following description, however, seeks to indicate in terms which are broadly reliable the essentials in the Anabaptist view of the church.

The great Reformers—Luther, Zwingli, Calvin—had tremendous regard for the living tradition of the historic Church. They had no urge to unchurch themselves, nor, indeed, any valid reason to suppose they had done so. As they saw it, the existing Church was indeed the true church, but it had fallen on evil days and into unworthy hands. The problem, therefore, was how to achieve its moral and spiritual renewal from within, so as to vindicate its place in history and render it usable in the hand of God. That in undertaking such a program a great breach should be made in the life of the church on its institutional side was regrettable, but in no way did it sever the Reformers from their sense of relation to historic Christianity. It was papal Rome, they concluded, which had departed the faith and forsaken charity.

The Anabaptist agitation began on this very point, and it began in centers of the Reform. The "left wing" sense of churchmanship, with the exception of the "spirituals," was as high as that of Rome, Wittenberg, or Zürich. (Geneva was in a class by itself.) But more than this, the left wing understanding of the church plowed deeper than Rome's, Wittenberg's, and Zürich's, even while it reached as high. For while the Reformers maintained the principle of the territorial church—parish or national—and sought to reform that church with a freshly discovered gospel, the Anabaptists, discarding entirely the principle of a *Landeskirche* or *Volkskirche*, would restore a long-lost apostolic church pattern with the gospel. From the Anabaptist point of view, the difference between the Reformers and themselves was the difference between reform and restitution.

As the Anabaptists saw it, the task for sixteenth-century Christians was nothing else than the reconstitution of the true church itself, restoring that which had lapsed rather than reforming that which had erred. It was this impulse to restoration, more than any other idea or fact, which tended to unify the otherwise diverse parties of the left.[2] Only the restoration of a church which had, in reality, long since ceased to exist was adequate to God's demand and the need of the times. The Church of Rome—and the church of the Reformation, insofar as it remained a territorial or parish church—could not vindicate its place in history or be usable in God's scheme. The rift, therefore, between Reformers and Restorers could only widen, and the feud which followed was more intense because it was internecine. When the smoke of conflict had cleared, what had been vaguely surmised, but not fully defined, was confirmed as of first importance: There was a basic difference between the Reformers' and the Restorers' view of the church. The real problem, therefore, was not the act of baptism but mutually exclusive conceptions of the church.[3] The difference in interpretation of the "subject" of baptism only served to highlight the irreconcilability of the two views of the church.

[2] *Ibid.*, p. 50 f.
[3] *Ibid.*, p. 29.

What, then, Dr. Littell began with as a working hypothesis emerges as, in fact, the essence of the matter: *"The Anabaptists proper were those in the 'Left Wing' who gathered and disciplined a 'True Church' (rechte Kirche) upon an apostolic pattern."* [4] Common agreement among Anabaptists as to the sum total of elements requisite to the full life of the "true" church, did not, however, immediately appear. The urgencies of their immediate situation (persecution without; trial and error within), plus the diversity of the influences which played upon the beginnings of their life (Erasmus, the Reformers, and Joachim of Flora, among others), made immediate agreement among them well-nigh impossible. Actually, on the view of the church, one needs to distinguish three parties of the left wing.

Using ecclesiology as the norm, the "left-wing of the left wing" was the party of the "Spirituals," led by highly individualistic leaders like Hans Denck, Caspar Schwenkfeld, and Sebastian Frank. This group moved on beyond "Anabaptism proper," somewhat in the same fashion as "Anabaptism proper" moved on beyond state-church Reform. The "spirituals" stressed the "inner word," the "new age of the Spirit," and "nonsectarianism." Their *summum bonum* was freedom. Such things as acceptance of the authority of the written Word, emphasis upon believer's baptism, or the enforcement of congregational discipline, were—to use a phrase of Schwenkfeld—a "new captivity to conscience."

The "right-wing of the left wing"—in ecclesiology—was the party of the revolutionaries, led at first by such men as Münzer and Karlstadt, and later by Hofmann, Matthys, and, for a time, by Hans Hut. This party stressed prophetic chiliasm and deliberately provoked social revolt. In a way they were not Anabaptists at all. The revolutionaries and the

[4] *Ibid.,* p. 50.

"spirituals" were actually close kin in their low estimate of the organized church and, for that matter, apparently, in their social hope. They differed mainly as to the means of realizing that hope. These two were the fringes of Anabaptism; or, as Littell has put it, they represent the "centrifugal forces" of the left wing.

Still using ecclesiology as the norm, the "center of the left wing" may be called "Anabaptism proper," and this was the party whose life was transmitted in Mennonitism and related groups to posterity. This group stressed responsible discipleship (rejecting the baptism of infants who had not "come" to baptism but who had been "brought") and group discipline (a gathered congregation, rather than the ecclesiastical institution of a given territory). Strictly speaking, this group repudiated subjectivism as the principle of Christian truth and condemned revolution as the method of Christian action. This means specifically that Anabaptists proper were neither mystics nor revolutionaries. Even the early emphasis on the individual conscience was gradually subordinated to the concept of group discipline, and full congregational autonomy seems to have been considered of essential importance only by the Hübmaier group at Waldshut. This "gathered church" would make its way in the world by triumphant suffering and prophetic witnessing.

Much of the modern confusion as to the nature of Anabaptism derives from the fact that its first opponents—such as Luther, Melanchthon, Bullinger, and Menius—themselves confused the outer fringees with the main group and attributed abuses to the whole movement which were characteristic only of the smaller part. Luther's frequent attacks on the *Schwärmer* ("fanatics," an epithet for all parties named above without distinction) stress, first, their individualistic subjectivism as subversive of a properly organized church and, second, their social violence as destructive of established order. It is now evident that Luther and the others made only a one-sided interpretation of the whole movement, based on groups which were on the fringe and were minor in number. Although he did not recognize it, the center majority party of Anabaptists was emphasizing matters which Luther himself had earlier stressed, the Christian's life of personal faith and the congregation's need for discipline. The chief difference, therefore, between Luther and the party of the center, the "Anabaptists proper," would seem to have stemmed from this: That for Luther the unity of the evangelical movement was more important than the principle of the regenerate organized church, and for the Anabaptists the principle of the regenerate organized church was more important than the unity of the evangelical movement. Further, Luther never saw (1) that the individualistic principle of the "Spirituals" would be as subversive to the center group of Anabaptists as to Lutheranism and (2) that political revolution was foreign to such Anabaptists as Grebel, Manz, Reublin, Blaurock, and Menno Simons as definitely as it was foreign to Luther himself. Note the fact that the acceptance of the "Spiritual" principle would as quickly undermine a voluntary association as a state church. And it is a further fact that pacifists are not revolutionaries.

The meaning of the terms "fall" and "restitution" as applied to the church is important for understanding the Anabaptists. For the fact of "fall" was the occasion for "restitution."

The idea of the "fall" is related to a primitivist note in Anabaptist life, which stressed a "golden age of the faith," when martyr-heroes followed Christ to death. In that age, so the interpretation ran with general correctness, Christians refused to bear arms, held goods in common, practiced a vigorous simplicity, and in all things were separated from the world and unto God. The "fall" from this high plane may be variously dated or explained according to the special emphasis of the one using the idea as a device for interpreting church history. Thus while Luther and Zwingli would date the "fall" in the Middle Ages and see the Constantinian revolution as something of a "social triumph of the early church," the restitution party, in the main, dated the "fall" from Constantine. For the majority this meant a "fall" through a union of church and state. The effecting of such union was to involve an encroachment by the state on the spiritual realm. This led, in turn, to what were considered to be basic denials of the Christian way, such as the killing of fellow beings at the command of the magistrate or frivolous conformity to cultural convention.

The means by which this illicit union of church and state was perpetuated was the rite of infant baptism. It was by flooding the church with hordes of nominal Christians that the "fall" was introduced. Then by including children en masse in baptism, rather than one at a time by conversion of life, the "fall" was perpetuated. Since the very nature of the Christian confession had meaning only in the context of inner faith and commitment, the confessional and initiatory rite could not be administered to preresponsible infants or children. And, further, it was for this same reason that a Christian congregation, as a voluntary fellowship not coterminous with the civil community, must be free of state control.

The church, however, must be a "voluntary association," not in order to glorify an ultimately egocentric individualism, but in order to be free to follow the New Testament pattern and to reproduce the original quality of New Testament life. This is to say that Anabaptism saw the necessity for its organized life to be free *from* the state in order that it might be free *unto* God. The demonstration of one's freedom as being unto God was the only justification for his being free from the state.

On the one side, then, "restitution" could be effected wherever those historic perversions were eliminated which had caused the "fall": union with the state, unregenerate membership of which infant baptism was both a vivid sign and secondary cause, and hierarchical displacement of personal religious responsibilities and prerogatives. On the other side, restitution was considered to have been accomplished wherever churches were gathered on the principle of responsible faith and regenerate life (of which believer's baptism is the sign but not the cause); whenever congregations were spiritually governed and cohered on the principle of mutual nurture and mutual rebuke; whenever the terms of communion were essentially moral and ethical rather than sacramental (with the sacraments being primarily symbols of a communion between the church and God, and between believer and believers). With the whole gospel in every believer, and with the whole church in every congregation, the beauty and grandeur of that "true" church, which was thought to have been "without spot and blemish," has been recaptured.

There was something here, it is evident, other than what one finds in either the party of the Reformation or among the "spiritualists." But more was involved in the "restitution" than a mere restoration of the past. The reconstitution of apostolic life was related to a future victory of God. That is to say: the gathering of a church of the restitution was itself a foretaste and pledge of the final restoration of all things by an act of God. The Christian, in the interim, was to be separated from the world in order to be related redemptively to the world. His way was the way of suffering

and witness. This leads directly to the next point: The Anabaptist view of the church controls and determines the view
of the Christian's relationship to society.

The Anabaptist View of the Church and the Christian's Relationship to Society

The Anabaptists had not only the vision of a disciplined
community of faith but, as well, the vision of a corporate
body in which Christ would take up habitation by the
Spirit and through which he would reign in the world. The
distinctiveness of their view may perhaps best be shown by
comparing it with the Lutheran and the Calvinistic views.

The Lutheran ethic—according to the common interpretation—stressed man's vertical relationship in the Christian life
more than his horizontal. Man's sins were freely forgiven,
he was justified by faith, his destiny was sealed. In the inner
disposition he forsook the things of this world, and in society
he performed the duties appropriate to his status or calling.
The social order as such would remain non-Christian. The
Reformed ethic carried a more radical program for society.
The social order *as such* was to be a positive vehicle for ex-
pressing, and an institution for establishing, Christian truth.
Government, as truly as home and church, was a divine institution. All its offices, high and low, were to be filled by
Christians and used for kingdom ends.

On this subject the Anabaptists represent a position which
combined, in a distinctive way, elements which the remainder
of the Protestant tradition kept separate. The Anabaptists
were not looking for the redemption of the social order any
more than the Lutherans were. Yet the goal of a Christian
society was as constantly before them as before the eyes of
the Reformed. The clue to this apparent *non sequitur* was
the Anabaptists' view of the church. These Christians would

be separate from the state and from the world precisely because both realms lay—and would always lie—in the "evil one." But they would as realistically demonstrate God's rule in the world as any theocracy might ever attempt. This rule of God in Christ—the "kingdom"—found concrete embodiment in the church. In their fellowship the kingdom *had* come. The Christian society was to be sought and realized and extended within the church.[5] "The church of Christ was therefore the society in which Christ exercised His glorious reign. The highest achievement of this life was to participate in extending that kingdom of glory." [6]

The actual performance of Christianity in this world and on these terms required a separation from the world in order to make redemptive contact with the world. The world was lost. But men might be won from the world and unto God. The society of those thus won, the saving salt in a decaying world, was the church of Jesus Christ. This involved for the church a heroic independence of this world's goods. It involved what Ernst Troeltsch called an *innerweltliche Askese*, an asceticism carried on in the world. This type of moral heroism is as earnest as monasticism on the principle of renunciation, but it does not physically forsake the order of society which it morally renounces. This kind of ethical separation—which is an implementation of faith and not a legalization of morality—can be sustained only where the community of believers will both pay the price of its separation and, at the same time, not surrender its task. The world will tolerate nothing so little as nonconformity: the Anabaptist Christian knew, therefore, that he must be prepared to *suffer*. Yet this world of intolerant humanity is, equally with the be-

[5] Cf. John C. Wenger, *Glimpses of Mennonite History and Doctrine* (Scottdale, Pa.: Herald Press, 1949), pp. 169–172.
[6] *Ibid.*, p. 170.

liever, the object of God's redeeming purpose: the Anabaptist Christian must therefore be prepared to *witness*. In a profound sense the two were often one. The price to pay was suffering. The task to perform was witnessing. By the thousands, in one of the most selfless endeavors in the church's history, the Anabaptists suffered for the privilege of bearing the witness. Such was their relation to society, and the relation is one which is implied in their distinctive view of the nature of the church.

The primitivist note in Anabaptist life, mentioned above, relates also at the point of the Christian's suffering. The early church made its way in a pagan world without recourse to armed might, and this in the face both of popular outbreaks of hostility and of government-sponsored persecution. Christianity was "no child's play." One must gird oneself for battle even with "principalities and powers" and stand fast, "and having done all, still to stand." The warfare must be waged. Whoever would wear the crown must manfully contend. Christ's example of "obedience unto death" both became a type of the disciple's suffering and lent divine significance to it. The Christian's warfare is a warfare waged with spiritual weapons. He must, therefore, be strong to stand when the enemy's counterattack is mounted with weapons which kill the body. The Christian's indispensable virtue, then, must be long-suffering. That is, he must be slow to retaliate and patient to endure in the face of abuse.

The church, it appears plainly from this, is a martyr-church. Her place in history is vindicated in terms of her patient suffering. The church is no better than was her Lord. The Anabaptists thus developed a theology of suffering, in terms of which the persecuted remnant became the triumphant church. The *eschaton* was already sure because there was a foretaste of final victory in the salvation already experienced. The very baptismal rite by which men entered the redeemed community was interpreted by many as a sign of salvation through suffering. No Anabaptist could ignore the possibility of martyrdom.

This new martyr, like his Lord, had "not where to lay his head." He lived "loose from the world." His was often the way of pilgrimage in the most literal sense. The clue indeed to the wide diffusion of Anabaptism in its early stages is this enforced mobility of the leadership through persecution. This mobility was not at first a deliberate strategy. Rather, Anabaptist leaders, where they had gone seeking peace from persecution, would be led to gather and shepherd little flocks of the faithful. This is the historical fact which first revealed the connection between the suffering life and the life of witnessing. It was only later that deliberate evangelistic or missionary strategy developed from the effects of persecution on the wandering pilgrims.

No Scripture passage had more use in Anabaptist circles than Matthew 28:19-20, the Great Commission. The charge to go into all the world applied to the simple craftsman as well as to the scholar, to the peasant as well as to the prince. When men were admitted by baptism into Anabaptist congregations, they were confronted with the moral necessity of becoming missionary pilgrims, should the occasion and the Spirit join to lead that way. Baptism came to be understood, therefore, not only as a sign of salvation through suffering, as said above, but as well a commission to missionary witnessing. The Great Commission in Matthew anticipated that as men went, they should preach the gospel, provoke faith, and baptize those who believed. These baptized believers were nurtured on Christ's teaching, builded into the community of faith, and, in turn, were to go out to repeat for others the process by which the gospel had come to them.

The proper order of the process could not be missed. The gospel was first to be preached. Men were, on the basis of this gospel, to believe unto salvation. They were then, and only then, to be baptized. The congregation into which they were brought was made up of folk, each of whom had made responsible commitment of life and confession of faith, and each of whom was now commissioned to bear witness of the gospel to others. The whole world was the field. The Anabaptists, without comprehensive organization, began quite naturally and worked outward from where they were. These witnesses may thus be appropriately described, with Professor Kenneth Scott Latourette, as the "forerunners" of the modern missionary movement.

The continuing integrity of such a movement as Anabaptism would obviously depend on the strength of its internal discipline. For those who were genuinely ready to go anywhere under any circumstances with the gospel—an incredibly high percentage of the whole—the spiritual quality of the movement would, automatically, take precedence over its numerical size. Further, where a husband and father knew that in case of his own execution for heresy his wife and children would be cared for by his fellow believers, he could be much readier in his commitment to go anywhere any time with the gospel. It is for this reason, as Littell pointed out, that the period of most ardent missionary passion coincided with the period of strongest internal discipline. This is a fact which Christians who now adhere to the congregational principle ought to reassess in relation to present circumstances.

An eschatological element of importance appears in all this theology of suffering and missionary action. These witnesses were forerunners of "a time to come." God's mighty saving arm was about to be revealed to all peoples. This was the faith not only of the revolutionaries but also of the pacifists. Both had seen the coming fulfilment; they were in disagreement as to the nature of man's co-operation with its coming. But in any case, in the suffering of each believer appeared something of what was "lacking of the sufferings of Christ." In the gathering of each new congregation was seen an approximation of the final fulfilment. In the "world" was nought but tribulation, but whoever knew Christ could be of good cheer through his victory over the world. The "true" church, the church of the restitution, the pilgrim-missionary-martyr church, is always proscribed and persecuted. But he who makes war on evil with the Sword of the Spirit and joins his Master in suffering for the will of God is *already* participating in the final victory. This is the nature of history and the clue to its meaning. This is also the corporate Christian life of fellowship and service within which the reign of God has come and from which the believer makes redemptive approach to the world.

Conclusion

The indirect influence of the Anabaptist movement is perhaps more comprehensively significant than the numerical strength of its direct lineage would suggest. Institutionally, Anabaptism has been directly perpetuated by the Mennonites and Hutterian Brethren. The influence of the "left wing," however, is very large upon all modern—and especially American—Christianity.

Contrary to an erroneous popular notion, the Baptist movement is not a continuation of Continental Anabaptism (with a dropping of the prefix "Ana-"). The Baptists who emerged for the first time in seventeenth-century England did have some historical antecedents. These included: (1) Lollardism, which had never ceased to affect the temper of English ecclesiastical life; (2) Calvinism, both in its strict and Arminian forms, which was to be the major theological anvil on which Baptist doctrine was hammered out; and (3) Dutch Anabaptism, which was to leave its mark by emigration in large numbers from Holland to England, especially in coastal England where Baptist life was first to appear. There is no succession between Baptists and Anabaptists in the institutional sense, nor is there unanimity of faith and practice as touching all the principles of the faith. Neither is it beside the point to remember that one main motif in the Anabaptist witness was precisely that *there was no institutional succession in history* to the "regularity" of which they could appeal or to which they could be joined.

Rather than being simply an extension of Anabaptism, the English Baptist movement must be construed as one way the gospel expressed itself in the context of ecclesiastical and social life in the early seventeenth century. Understanding the Baptist position of that time involves knowing the historical development from Anglicanism per se to Puritanism, from Puritanism to Separatism, and from Separatism to Baptist congregations.

The chief likeness of an early English or American Baptist congregation to a Continental Anabaptist one lies in the common acceptance of the principle of the gathered and disciplined church. In the early Baptist tradition there was little if any idea of "spiritualistic individualism." The church was visible because it was a cohering group of regenerated believers already embodying and manifesting the "Catholick Church." But this "catholic church" was identical with no single ecclesiastical organization. To affirm such identity, as when any one ecclesiastical structure claims to be "*the* church," would—on early Baptist principles—amount to blasphemy. Further, the church stood under the Word of God and not under subjectivistic whim. It maintained its integrity by mutual nurture and the apostolic use of the ban. There was separation from the state because the church was regenerate, while the state was the legal structure of that order which lay in the "evil one."

On Baptist principles, if not always in Baptist practice, it is of little moment to have a token separation of church and state on the organizational level but only a little cleavage between the church and the "world" at the level of motives and goals. When, for example, church membership involves no relation among believers which determines their attitudes and relations in the world and to the world, a Baptist church in any historic sense is an impossibility. Baptists cannot affirm as primary any principle which is subordinated to something else. Thus if regional mores are more determinative of *religious* alignments than is the fellowship of believers in the gospel, it is because such folkways are ultimately either more precious or more powerful for church members than is the gospel. No Baptist church can fully be a Christian fellowship in the New Testament sense if it accepts the role of the religious institution for a given race or class in a given area and permits its range of fellowship and common life to be determined by customs rather than by faith in Christ through the gospel. Neither can such a church claim spiritual succession with Continental Anabaptism or with early English Baptists.

One's doctrine of the church must obviously be constructed out of those materials which are thought relevant, and therefore authoritative, for such doctrinal construction. Baptists have consistently professed to find in the Scriptures their court of final doctrinal appeal. This is good. But the Bible requires interpretation. No proof-text method of using the Bible can properly be called a "biblical" method. One must, rather, study the Bible in its original setting and interpret

its various parts in relation to their original occasion and purpose. Circumstantial and peripheral elements must be distinguished from essential and central elements. Even essential
elements must be balanced against each other in order to work
out a system of doctrines, for biblical narratives usually do
not strive for an over-all balance but rather emphasize a particular truth in view of an immediate need. For in the biblical
accounts doctrine as such is more usually presupposed than
elaborated. This is as it should be. In the Bible the immediacy
of revelation is confronting man, eliciting his personal response
and being apprehended in experience. That same immediacy
ought still to be apprehended in the experience of believers
through the Holy Spirit. But Baptists have never believed
the Spirit apart from the Word. They turn, therefore, to
Scripture and seek to gain comprehensive understanding of
its meaning and implication for life. Making consistent use
of its teachings thus requires a systematic ordering of its
contents. If one wants to state *all* that the Bible teaches on
a given subject, such systematic treatment is necessary. Only
in this way does doctrine emerge as genuinely biblical.

This point may be illustrated from the New Testament
with respect to the doctrine of the church. In Galatians and
Romans the church appears, in the main, as "the congregation of the faithful." This view of the church gives primacy
to the preaching of the word and to worship through Scripture, baptism, and the Supper. In 1 Corinthians and Ephesians
the church appears, in the main, as "the body of Christ."
The Christian life appears here as mutual incorporation into
the life of the body. This view gives stress to apostolic representation and to the problems of order. In Acts the church
appears, in the main, as "the fellowship of the Spirit." This
sees the church wherever the Spirit is present with power and
finds the distinctiveness of the faith in the ontological change

which it produces in the believer. This is stressed in Acts much more than, for example, the problem of order or doctrinal orthodoxy. To be sure, these three types are not mutually exclusive.

No doctrine of the church is adequate which neglects any one of these three emphases. This is because all three are unquestionably biblical. Lesslie Newbigin has recently written a fine study of the church in which these three emphases are denominated respectively, the Protestant, the Catholic (obviously not Roman Catholic), and the Pentecostal (not the denomination of that name).[7]

In what we are here calling "the center of the left wing," *i.e.*, in Anabaptism proper, one is reasonably close to a balanced embodiment in history of the "Protestant," "Catholic," and "Pentecostal" emphases.

Only the church which is "the congregation of believers," "the body of Christ," and "the fellowship of the Spirit" is the New Testament church. And only that church which stands under the word and Spirit of God in a repenting faith and believing repentance can give humble and courageous witness to a gospel which is God's answer to anyone's life because it is God's answer to everyone's life. Under the word and Spirit the church's faith may become redemptive in all life's relationships and her fellowship become as generous as is the love of the God she worships.[8]

[7] Lesslie Newbigin, *The Household of God* (New York: Friendship Press, 1954).

[8] The following is a simple list of readings designed to amplify the perspectives of this essay and to deal with numerous matters not treated here, but which are of basic importance. One may find the *Schleitheim Confession* and *Dordrecht Confession* (both Anabaptist) in John C. Wenger, *Glimpses of Mennonite History and Doctrine* (Scottdale, Pa.: Herald Press, 1949), pp. 206–228. Certain other Anabaptist and Mennonite statements serve as introduction to the Baptist ones in W. J. McGlothlin,

Baptist Confessions of Faith (Philadelphia: American Baptist Publication Society, 1911), pp. 1–49.

Besides Littell's, *The Anabaptist View of the Church,* and the two volumes mentioned in the above paragraph, two others will be of great value for understanding the subject of this essay: Harold S. Bender, *Conrad Grebel, c. 1498-1526, The Founder of the Swiss Brethren sometimes called Anabaptists* (Goshen, Indiana: The Mennonite Historical Society, 1950); and John C. Wenger, *Introduction to Theology* (Scottdale, Pa.: Herald Press, 1954).

VII

THE BEGINNINGS OF BAPTIST CHURCHES

Robert G. Torbet

BAPTISTS TODAY are Christians who are distinguished by an evangelical Protestant faith, which they hold in common with their brethren of other communions, and by certain principles which have come to be marks of their distinctive contribution to the body of Christ. These include the following: (1) a belief that the Bible constitutes the only authority for faith and practice in the Christian life; (2) a conviction that a personal experience of the regenerative work of the Holy Spirit in one's life is a prerequisite of church membership; (3) the practice of believer's baptism, which is baptism of an individual who is able and willing to make his own profession of faith in Jesus Christ as his Lord and Saviour; (4) an adherence to the scriptural teaching of the priesthood of believers, which is the spiritual principle underlying their democratic type of church life; and (5) an intense loyalty to the principle of religious liberty, which is founded upon the scriptural teaching of the individual's responsibility to God alone for his eternal destiny.

No one disputes the fact that there have been Baptists in this sense from the beginning of the seventeenth century. However, there is great difference of opinion concerning the existence of people of this persuasion prior to that time. For example, the Baptists of the seventeenth century, who were

English-speaking, were insistent that they were not to be confused with the Anabaptists, whose origins were European and who were identified with the radical left wing of the Protestant Reformation on the continent of Europe. The little English congregation of Baptists, organized under the leadership of John Smyth in Amsterdam, Holland, in 1608 or 1609, complained that the term "Anabaptist" was used unjustly as a name of reproach against them. For more than a century this was a common refrain in Baptist confessional statements and other writings.

For instance, the General Baptists, in their Confession of 1611, listed the distinctive Anabaptist doctrines as errors and in 1660 set forth a formal statement of their beliefs under the heading, "A Brief Confession or Declaration of Faith, Set forth by many of us, who are (falsely) called Ana-Baptists." [1] In a similar manner, the Particular or Calvinistic Baptists included this note in their confessional statement in 1644: "The Confession of Faith, Of those churches which are commonly (though falsly [sic]) called Anabaptists." [2]

In addition to such protestations against any identification with Anabaptists, the English Baptists firmly rejected many Anabaptist teachings and practices. Among these were the Anabaptists' aversion to oathtaking, holding public office, military service, and going to court, as well as certain theological views which included the doctrine of soul sleeping, the insistence that Christ did not receive his humanity from Mary, the rejection of the doctrine of original sin, and belief in the necessity of an apostolic succession in the administration of baptism. Concerning the latter point, a further word of explanation may be in order. The phrase "apostolic suc-

[1] W. J. McGlothlin, *Baptist Confessions of Faith* (Philadelphia: American Baptist Publication Society, 1911), pp. 85–93, 111.
[2] *Ibid.*, p. 171.

cession in the administration of baptism" is used here for want of a better term to describe the insistence that New Testament, or believer's, baptism should be received from those who in turn have received it themselves.

The theological orientation of the English Baptists has recently been described by Professor Winthrop S. Hudson, a Baptist historian:

Far from deriving their theology from the humanists of the Northern Renaissance as was true of the Anabaptists, the Baptists were children of the Reformation and stood clearly within the Calvinist tradition. This fact is sufficiently apparent in all the early confessions, but it is made explicit by the action of the Particular Baptists in 1677—following the lead of the Congregationalists—in adopting with only slight modifications, as a statement of their own theological views, the Presbyterian Westminster Confession of Faith. It was this slightly altered Westminster Confession which became, with the addition of two articles dealing with the singing of Psalms and the laying on of hands, the Philadelphia Confession of Faith of the American Baptists. While the General Baptists did not reproduce the Westminster Confession, the so-called "Orthodox Creed," which they adopted in 1679, was scarcely less Calvinistic. It affirmed their belief in original sin, and the articles dealing with the church are sufficient to banish all question as to the particular tradition in which they stood.[3]

[3] Winthrop S. Hudson, "Baptists Were Not Anabaptists," *The Chronicle*, Vol. XVI, No. 4 (Oct., 1953), p. 172.

The articles of the 1679 creed which deal with the church, read as follows:

"There is one holy catholick church, consisting of, or made up of the whole number of the elect . . . which church is gathered by special grace, and the powerful and internal work of the spirit; and are effectually united unto Christ, their head, and can never fall away.

"Nevertheless, we believe the visible church of Christ on earth, is made up of several distinct congregations, which make up that one catholick church, or mystical body of Christ. And the marks by which she is known to be the true spouse of Christ, are these, vis. Where the word of God is rightly preached, and the sacraments truly administered, according to Christ's institution, and the practice of the primitive church; having

Further evidence of this orientation of English Baptists in the direction of Calvinistic doctrine rather than of Mennonite teaching may be seen in the great popularity of Benjamin Keach's Catechism, widely used after its issuance in the late seventeenth century. It seems that this appeared after 1689 when the Baptist Confession of 1677 (an alteration of the Westminster Confession of 1648 to suit Baptist views of the church and its ordinances) was reviewed and adopted by the first General Assembly of Particular Baptists of England and Wales, held in London in September. Keach's work was largely an adaptation of the Westminster Shorter Catechism, modified at two or three points to conform to congregational polity and the Baptist doctrine of believer's baptism. Its author was a former General Baptist who, like several of his contemporary ministers in the vicinity of London, had become a Calvinist.

Although many opponents of their position sought to discredit seventeenth-century English Baptists on the grounds that they were "Anabaptists," there were some who recognized and admitted that the charge was unfounded. Among these was Richard Baxter, who described the Baptists in his *Autobiography* (published posthumously in 1696) as "sober, godly people" who "differed from others but in the point of infant-baptism (the Particular Baptists), or at most in the points of predestination, and free will, and perseverance (the General or Arminian Baptists)." In 1644 Daniel Neal reported that the Baptists were Calvinistic in doctrine and Independent (Congregational) in discipline.[4]

---

discipline and government duly executed, by ministers or pastors of God's appointing, and the church's election, that is a true constituted church; to which church, and not elsewhere, all persons that seek for eternal life, should gladly join themselves" (McGlothlin, *op. cit.*, pp. 145–46.).

[4] Cited in editorial supplement to the 1844 edition of Daniel Neal, *History of the Puritans*, Vol. III.

Thomas Crosby, whose *History of the English Baptists from the Reformation to the Beginning of the Reign of King George I* was published in 1738–40, appears to have been the first Baptist historian to attempt to demonstrate the existence of Baptist churches from apostolic times to his own day. He sought, therefore, to show that Baptists stood in a line of spiritual succession with at least some of the more moderate Anabaptist groups. Although he was unsuccessful in proving his thesis conclusively, he did blur for future generations the distinctions which had existed between Anabaptists and his people. In commenting on this point, Professor Hudson has written:

A century later, when the former sturdy Calvinism (whether in its Arminian or more orthodox form) of the Baptists had been replaced by a vague evangelicalism so that Baptists were no longer equipped to make careful theological distinctions, Crosby's hesitant identification of Baptists and Anabaptists was accepted and elaborated with scarcely a reservation, and became a standard feature of Baptist apologetics.[5]

Those who took this position were: (1) G. H. Orchard, an English Baptist minister, who in 1855 wrote *A Concise History of Foreign Baptists;* (2) J. M. Cramp, professor in Acadia College in Nova Scotia, who in 1868 wrote a *Baptist*

[5] Hudson, *op. cit.,* p. 178. Professor Hudson, in this view, has challenged the assumption that Arminianism was a revolt against Calvinism. According to his interpretation, Arminians considered themselves to be within the Calvinistic tradition. They intended to provide a corrective to the extremes of Calvinistic teaching with respect to a limited atonement and divine election. This view is implied by Ernst Troeltsch *The Social Teaching of the Christian Churches,* trans. Olive Wyon (New York: Macmillan Co., 1931), II, 683–86. John T. McNeill, of Union Theological Seminary in New York, has suggested that Arminius and his followers, the Remonstrants, were in closer accord with Calvin's position than the hyper-Calvinists of the Synod of Dort that condemned them. See *Makers of Christianity: from Alfred the Great to Scheiermacher* (New York: Henry Holt & Co., 1935), p. 222.

History: from the Foundations of the Christian Church to the Close of the Eighteenth Century; (3) William Cathcart, editor of *The Baptist Encyclopedia*, published in 1881; and (4) John T. Christian, professor in the Baptist Bible Institute (now New Orleans Baptist Seminary) in New Orleans, Louisiana, who wrote in 1922 a two-volume work entitled *A History of the Baptists.*[6]

Some who admit the difficulty of establishing any historical connection between the long line of reforming sects during medieval and Reformation days (such as the Donatists, Novatians, Henricians, Petrobrusians, Waldensians, and the German, Dutch, and Swiss Anabaptists) advance what may be called the spiritual kinship theory. According to this point of view, there has been maintained a succession of regenerated, baptized believers who have been true to the Baptist witness in these minority groups that had arisen in the centuries following the defection from New Testament Christianity. Among those who held this position have been: (1) David Benedict, author of *A General History of the Baptist Denomination in America and Other Parts of the World* (1848); (2) Richard B. Cook, who taught that there is a spiritual kinship between Baptists and Anabaptist sects in his book, *The Story of the Baptists in All Ages and Countries* (1884); (3) Thomas Armitage, who expresses his point of view in the title of his volume, *A History of the Baptists; Traced by Their Vital Principles and Practices, from the Time of Our Lord and Saviour Jesus Christ to the Year 1889* (1889); (4) Albert H. Newman, in his story of the Anabaptists, *A History of Anti-pedobaptism* (1897); and (5) Walter Rauschenbusch, of Rochester Baptist Theological Seminary, whose interest in the influence of social applications of the

[6] For details, see Robert G. Torbet, *A History of the Baptists* (Philadelphia: Judson Press, 1950), pp. 59–60.

gospel may have prompted his identification of the Baptists with the socially radical Anabaptists.[7]

Joseph Ivimey, author of *A History of English Baptists* (1811) in four volumes, may be regarded as the forerunner of still a third theory concerning the origin of Baptists. He held that the Baptist movement was English and had its roots in the various forms of English medieval dissent. In this was the hint of the more specific theory being advanced by many today, known as the English Separatist descent theory. Advocates of this viewpoint explain that Baptists originated with certain English Separatists who were congregational in their doctrine of the church and who had come to see the indefensible position of those who baptized infants while maintaining the concept of a gathered church. They therefore pursued the logical course of their thinking and rejected infant baptism, which was so intimately associated with a covenant idea of the church.

This position has been held in various forms by several Baptist historians in recent years. One variety of the theory was advanced in 1896 by William H. Whitsitt, professor at the Southern Baptist Theological Seminary in Louisville, Kentucky. He dated the origin of Baptist churches from 1641 when immersion was renewed in England by a few English Separatists who came out of the Jacob Church at Southwark, London. Great controversy surrounded the publication of his book entitled *A Question in Baptist History: Whether the Anabaptists in England Practiced Immersion Before the Year 1641?* Although he lost his position at the seminary, his viewpoint was endorsed by Augustus H. Strong, president of Rochester Baptist Theological Seminary, in a historical address delivered in 1904.

The noted Baptist churchman John Howard Shakespeare

[7] For details see *Ibid.*, p. 60.

set forth still another form of the theory at the turn of the century. He sought to demonstrate an unbroken Baptist witness through the Particular Baptists, arguing that the succession of old General Baptist churches, which had begun with Helwys' congregation at Spitalfield outside of London about 1612, had been broken by the defection of General Baptists into unitarianism and by the union of those who remained orthodox with the Particular Baptists in 1891.[8]

More recent English Baptist historians, W. T. Whitley and A. C. Underwood, have rejected the supposition that there is a connection between Anabaptists and Baptists. Their explanation instead is that the Baptists were indigenous to England and expressed the logical conclusions of the thinking of the English Separatists.[9]

Henry C. Vedder, American Baptist historian, reached the conclusion that there was undoubted documentary evidence for an unbroken succession of Baptist churches after 1610 and that "from about the year 1641, at latest, Baptist doctrine and practice have been the same in all essential features that they are to-day."[10] That the English Separatist descent theory is the most plausible to fit the facts is evident from a brief summary of the rise of English and American Baptist churches.[11]

The history of English Baptists begins in Holland with a religious refugee and his congregation who had come out of the Church of England on a spiritual pilgrimage toward the

[8] John H. Shakespeare, *Baptist and Congregational Pioneers* (London: National Council of Evangelical Free Churches, 1906), pp. 179–80.

[9] William T. Whitley, *A History of British Baptists* (London: C. Griffin & Co., Ltd., 1923), pp. 18–19; A. C. Underwood, *A History of the English Baptists* (London: Baptist Union Publication Department, Kingsgate Press, 1947), p. 27.

[10] Henry C. Vedder, *A Short History of the Baptists* (Philadelphia: American Baptist Publication Society, 1907), p. 201.

[11] For details, see Torbet, *op. cit.*, pp. 62 ff., 219 ff.

by dipping the body into the water, resembling burial and rising again." [12] Because immersion had been generally discontinued in the Church of England by 1600, Blunt, who understood the Dutch language, went to the Netherlands, apparently at the request of others interested in the subject, to visit the Rhynsburgers or Collegiants, a minority group of Mennonites at Rhynsburg, who practiced immersion. Some believe that his purpose was to receive baptism by immersion at their hands so that he might return to baptize others in the same manner.[13] An examination of Burrage's corrected reading of the Kiffin manuscript (which traces the history of the first English Particular Baptist congregation) would indicate, to the contrary, that Blunt went to Rhynsburg to seek counsel rather than baptism from the Collegiant Mennonites.

For example, the manuscript does not state that John Batte(n), an elder of the Collegiants, immersed him but only that he received Blunt kindly and gave him letters for the church at London. It is likely that this communication contained instructions concerning the administration of immersion. Hence, the record reads that "Mr. Blunt Baptized Mr. Blacklock thyt was a Teacher amongst them, & Mr. Blunt being Baptized, he & Mr. Blacklock Baptized thye rest of their friends that ware so minded, & many being added to them they increased much." [14] Thus it appears that Blunt baptized Blacklock and was baptized by him in turn, whereupon the two together baptized the rest. While the point is debatable, this view is supported by the fact that the Calvinistic Baptists likely would not have been inclined to accept baptism from the Arminian Collegiants.

[12] A. C. Underwood, *op. cit.*, p. 59.
[13] *Ibid.*
[14] Champlin Burrage, *The English Dissenters in the Light of Recent Research* (1550–1641) (2 vols.; Cambridge: University Press, 1912), II, 302–304; I, 330–335.

These early Baptist churches in England very soon developed associational relationships for fellowship and mutual strengthening. Although General or Arminian Baptists did not fraternize with Particular or Calvinistic Baptists, each group developed its own type of organizational connection. It followed in both cases the associational pattern for community protection which had been developed during the Civil Wars (1642–49) by Cromwell's New Model army. This consisted of "associations" in the several counties, to which each regiment sent representatives. Baptists, who had served in the army, later adapted the plan to their church life. Accordingly, local congregations banded themselves into "associations" which met on occasions for counsel and inspiration and which presented a united front as minority bodies before the government. Particular Baptists preferred a loose type of organization, whereas the General Baptists developed a more centralized plan which went so far as to combine associations into an annual assembly that was national in scope. By 1655 the title "association" was generally accepted among Baptists. Out of such early interchurch relations developed eventually a denominational consciousness.[15]

A further aspect of church life among early English Baptists was the ministry. Although they believed heartily that all Christians are priests before God and that there is no allowable distinction made in the New Testament which would result in a clergy separate from the laity, Baptists did recognize a ministry. Selection and ordination of candidates for the ministry were reserved for the congregation. Procedure in ordination was not without some confusion among Baptists in the seventeenth century. This was due in part to a concern not to violate their basic concept of a lay ministry by the practice of setting aside "gifted brethren" for special

[15] For details, see Torbet, *op. cit.,* pp. 72–73.

service through a laying on of hands by the elders. Because such a ceremony might be interpreted by some as endowing a man with an authority beyond the right of his office, some churches eliminated its use. When the hands of the elders were laid upon a candidate, the act was recognized as a confirmation of the ordination that was inherent in the call from God and its acceptance.

Some churches went so far as to "lay hands" upon all believers who came into church membership. This ceremony, which followed immediately upon baptism, gave expression to a conviction that all believers are *called* to witness in a general sense. There were other Baptists who recognized the validity of an ordination ceremony, although this was specifically limited to the pastorate to which the candidate had been called.

The degree of preparation which was expected of Baptist ministers varied with the leaders and the church members concerned. Men who had come from a background of the Church of England, Presbyterianism, or Independency (Congregationalism) were usually the advocates of a trained ministry. But the rank and file of early Baptists, drawn largely from humble origins, were not greatly concerned with education. Nor did these believe in a well-paid ministry. The all-too-frequent spirit of independency, which all but made a fetish of the autonomy of the local congregation, also hindered any possibility of strengthening the leadership through united organization. It is commendable, however, that the first Assembly of Particular Baptists, meeting in London in 1689, should express a concern to develop an able ministry and should establish a fund to help weak churches to support their ministers.[16]

[16] For details, see Torbet, *The Baptist Ministry: Then and Now* (Philadelphia: Judson Press, 1953), pp. 9–16.

The story of the beginnings of Baptist churches in America has been told many times. Here we have only space to point out that the first Baptist congregations in this country were established in Rhode Island, one at Providence by Roger Williams in 1639 and the other by John Clarke at Newport, possibly in 1638 or later (the lack of records before 1648 making this a moot question). Both of these men were of Separatist background in England and had come to Baptist views (Williams in this country and Clarke possibly while still in England) by the road taken by Smyth, Helwys, and Spilsbury. The Baptist churches planted in Massachusetts, Pennsylvania, and South Carolina in the late seventeenth century and in Virginia in the early eighteenth were all products of the expanding witness of Baptists from England or Wales or of those who were migrating from one part of the Colonies to another.

The development of Baptist church life in the American Colonies was not sufficiently different from that in England to warrant a detailed description here. Associational relationships between small and struggling congregations began as early as 1707, with the organization of the Philadelphia Baptist Association. The pattern followed was English, even to the adoption in 1742 of the London Confession of Particular Baptists of 1689.

The ministry for these churches came from several sources. The earliest were men like Roger Williams, who migrated from Great Britain. Others, as the Great Awakening stirred revival fires near the middle of the eighteenth century, came from the ranks of Congregationalists in New England. Some of them were able men like Hezekiah Smith and Isaac Backus. Then there were scores of heroic and self-sacrificing men like Shubael Stearns, Daniel Marshall, Jacob Bower, and Luke Williams, whose untiring zeal matched the rapid movement of the frontier westward. The vast majority who served the scattered congregations of rural America at the close of the eighteenth century were farmer-preachers, untrained but zealous exhorters to people everywhere to repent and receive the Saviour. And because they were of the plain people, the masses heard them gladly.

By way of summary, certain conclusions may be drawn from the data at hand. One is that the English Baptists had a Congregationalist-Calvinistic background and repudiated any connection with the Anabaptists during the first century of their history. Another is that the English Baptists' acceptance of believer's baptism was the logical expression of the Reformation emphasis upon the necessity for a personal faith and was in accord with the congregational concept of a gathered church. Underlying their thinking was the ever-present desire to develop a visible expression of New Testament church life. Furthermore, the concern of later Baptist historians to prove a "succession" of Baptist churches from apostolic times had led to a violation of historical facts on the one hand and to a perversion of the nonconformist ideal that is inherent within Baptist teaching on the other. Perhaps the most significant lesson to be gained from such an observation is that the Spirit must ever have pre-eminence over forms and organizations.

Moreover, the failure to recognize the Calvinistic theological orientation of Baptists rather than the Mennonite theological background has obscured a proper understanding of historic Baptist patterns of worship and church life and of attitudes on social and political issues. Indeed, this confusion has become for some a justification for abandoning a church life and witness which has been an important part of the reform tradition, that is to say, that the church is to bring the will of God to bear upon every aspect of life.

Finally, the early church life of Baptists was very fluid and informal. Purposefully, the churches kept formalism and organization to a minimum in order that the Holy Spirit might be free to work through every believer. To be sure, as demands upon the ministry and the churches grew, the polity became more elaborate. But always Baptists sought to preserve what they believed to be the essence of the nature of the church—a democratic fellowship of believers witnessing and serving in the name of Jesus Christ.

VIII

THE LANDMARK MOVEMENT IN THE SOUTHERN BAPTIST CONVENTION

John E. Steely

THE STORY of the Landmark movement in the Southern Baptist Convention may be told in three parts. First, it was a tendency toward high-church exclusiveness, appearing in the Convention under the influence of J. R. Graves during the latter half of the nineteenth century. Second, it was a schism in the Baptist fellowship about the close of that century, ostensibly over the methods of missionary work but actually due to a radical disagreement in the field of ecclesiology. Third, it is a flourishing force in the Convention in mid-twentieth century, evidenced in currents of thought, patterns of preaching, and organizational principles.

Old Landmarkism: What Is It?

The name of Landmarkism to describe a movement among Baptists arose after 1854 when, at the request of J. R. Graves, J. M. Pendleton of Kentucky wrote an essay which Graves published in tract form under the title, "An Old Landmark Reset." Graves, a Vermonter by birth who had come to Nashville, Tennessee, by way of Ohio and Kentucky, was pastor of the Second Baptist Church in Nashville and editor of *The Tennessee Baptist*. In 1851, in a statement known as

134

the "Cotton Grove Resolutions," Graves had raised the questions which were to be central to Pendleton's essay. Briefly stated, they are: (1) Can Baptists recognize those societies not organized according to the pattern of the Jerusalem church as churches of Christ? (2) Ought they to be called gospel churches, or churches in a religious sense? (3) Ought their ministers to be recognized as gospel ministers? (4) Is it not virtually a recognition of them as gospel ministers to invite them into the pulpits of Baptist churches? (5) Ought Baptists to call "brethren" those who profess Christianity but do not "have the doctrine of Christ and walk not according to his commandments?" Graves' negative answer to all these set the pattern for the movement later to be known as Old Landmarkism. He later offered this indirect testimony to what he conceived to be the essential nature of the movement:

I think it is no act of presumption in me to assume to know what *I* meant by the Old Landmarks, since I was the first man in Tennessee, and the first *editor* on this continent, who publicly advocated the policy of *strictly* and consistently *carrying out in our practice those principles which all true Baptists, in all ages, have professed to believe.*[1]*

Throughout the book which bore this testimony Graves marshaled his facts, axioms, inferences, and corollaries in fine array to distinguish between the "strict Baptists" (the Landmarkers) and the liberals (open communionists). He accepted the name "Old Landmarker" as a badge of honor since "those ancient Anabaptists, whom we alone represent in this age, were content to be called Cathari and Puritans, which terms mean the same as Old Landmarkers." [2]

[1] J. R. Graves, *Old Landmarkism: What Is It?* (Texarkana, Texas: Baptist Sunday School Committee, 1928), p. xiv.
[2] *Ibid.,* p. xiii.

A major emphasis of Graves which serves to identify the Landmarkism of his time relates to church succession, expressed in the claim of Baptists to this distinction and thus to their sole right to baptize and ordain, the baptisms and orders of other bodies being null and void. It is not, of course, a peculiarity of Landmarkers alone that they claim apostolic succession for Baptist churches. Other Baptists who are not Landmarkers believe that such a succession may be traced or at least may be inferred. It is rather the *a priori* method of establishing such a claim, with the dependence upon this succession for present-day validity of the ordinances, which distinguishes the Landmark view.

Baptists claim that they are successors to the "Witnesses of Jesus," who preserved the faith *once* delivered to the saints, and kept the ordinances as they were originally committed to the primitive Churches. They claim to be the lineal descendants of the martyrs who, for so many ages, sealed their testimony with their blood. They claim that they can trace the history of communities, essentially like themselves, back through the "wilderness," into which they were driven by the dragon, and the beast that succeeded to him, and the image of the beast, by *a trail of blood*, lighted up by a thousand stakefires, until that blood mingles with the blood of the apostles, and the Son of God, and John the Baptist.[3]

Although he did not say so in this connection, the weight of this debatable declaration for Graves is this: That without such a demonstrable succession today's churches are left in utter confusion, since they lack an assurance of their authorization to preach and to baptize. While he never put the whole weight of Baptists' right to exist upon this frail frame, he did use the absence of such evidence as his basis for denying

[3] J. R. Graves, *The Trilemma; or, Death by Three Horns* (Texarkana, Texas: Baptist Sunday School Committee, 1921), pp. 119–120.

the right of other "societies" to call themselves churches of Christ. It may be inferred that Graves would have rejected with categorical righteousness the later suggestion of President Whitsitt of the Southern Baptist Theological Seminary that the Baptists of England had made a "new start" with their baptism in the seventeenth century. Too much depended, from Graves' point of view, upon the premise of succession. A brief example of his argument in one matter will illustrate this conclusion.

In his *Trilemma* Graves demolished the claims of the Freewill Baptists to the name of "church" for their "societies" thus:

Baptist churches [*i.e.*, missionary Baptist churches] are either the true churches of Christ or they are not.

If they are true churches, then the Freewill Baptists are but sectaries, and without baptism or church membership, and their ministers unbaptized and without authority to baptize, because apostates, and excluded from the church of Christ.[4]

If missionary Baptist churches are not true churches of Christ, then they had no authority and could not administer baptism or a true ministry, and the first ministers of the Freewill Baptists, who had received their baptism from these missionary Baptists, were also lacking in the essentials of a true ministry. "Freewill Baptists can not answer this question yea or nay, without destroying themselves as churches—viz:

"Are the baptisms of Baptist churches valid?"[5]

Another distinctive part of Graves' ecclesiology, also an essential part of Landmarkism as he understood it, was his idea of the observance of the Lord's Supper. In order to stress the particular view which he held, he sought to work

[4] *Ibid.*, p. 188.
[5] *Ibid.*, p. 189. Cf. J. R. Graves and Jacob Ditzler, *The Graves-Ditzler: or, Great Carrollton Debate* (Memphis: Southern Baptist Publication Society, 1876), pp. 1050–1052.

out its implications in various areas of church life. He believed that the Supper should be observed only by the local church, with none but members of that local church participating. This position he sought to establish by two lines of argument: first, that the ordinances were committed to the churches and were observed strictly within the limits of the local church during the apostolic age; and, second, that the Supper "symbolizes church relations, *i.e.*, that all who jointly partake are members of the one and self-same church." [6] Thus Graves laid heavy and regular stress upon the aspects of ecclesiology which within the context of the Anglican communion would be recognized as high church principles. These elements will be evidenced more clearly in the discussion of the succeeding phases of Landmarkism as they came into being at the close of the nineteenth century.

The Landmark Schism

Landmarkism never died after it was brought to birth by Graves and his associates. It did, however, change its complexion in the ensuing years, and from about the year 1880 the question of mission methods became one of the distinguishing marks of the movement and thus one of the chief issues in Baptist ecclesiology.

This phase of Landmarkism was confined almost entirely to the Southwest.[7] In at least two states, Arkansas and Texas, personal rivalry and animosity contributed largely to what became decisive separations. These might otherwise have been minor disagreements on matters of method. It has been suggested that the schism might have been the outcome of the bitter personal battles between two strong antagonists,

[6] J. R. Graves, *The Lord's Supper a Church Ordinance* (Memphis: Southern Baptist Publication Society, 1928), p. 15.

[7] A. H. Newman, *A History of Baptist Churches in the United States* (New York: The Christian Literature Co., 1894), p. 495.

each seeking to gain a dominant position in a relatively young situation. J. S. Rogers [8] has pointed out that no such strong movement of Landmarkism arose in the older and more mature states and conventions. He further noted that while the actual division took place in Arkansas, Texas, and Oklahoma, most of the Landmark leaders came from Kentucky, Tennessee, and Georgia. In fact, not one of the early leaders of the Landmark association in Arkansas was a native of that state.

For some years prior to 1900 the Arkansas Baptist State Convention had employed, through its Executive Board, a corresponding secretary (the title was not uniformly used) to promote the missionary work of the convention. The minutes of the meeting at Hope in 1900 tell of the election of A. J. Barton to fill the post, after W. E. Atkinson had been chosen and had declined. According to some students, it was the thwarted ambition of another aspirant to the office that then began the agitation which was to embroil all the Baptists of Arkansas for the next decade. The actual dispute arose, however, over the cost and the control of the missionary enterprise as it was then being carried on. In the 1900 meeting an attempt was made to change the system of mission work, but the supporters of the established program won a clear victory. The following year saw an intensified struggle over the same issue, but the 1901 meeting in Paragould ended with the convention plan still in effect. This was accomplished in spite of the fact that most of the messengers had come to the meeting opposed to the secretary, and many of them had been instructed by their churches to vote to abolish that post. Less than six months after this convention, in the spring of 1902, members of the defeated group met at Antioch Baptist

[8] J. S. Rogers, *History of Arkansas Baptists* (Little Rock: Arkansas Baptist State Convention, 1948), pp. 590 ff.

Church, in the suburbs of Little Rock, and formed the General Association of Baptists.

The separation was not yet final, and it was not considered final by those who took this drastic step, for they reappeared in the meetings of the convention and in the associations which had gone on record in opposition to their proposals. In the convention meeting of 1902, at Conway, a "peace committee" was appointed to meet with a like committee from the association for the purpose of seeking a settlement. During the succeeding year these committees held separate meetings and corresponded at length but never met jointly. An attitude of suspicion was evident in all their correspondence,[9] and it is not surprising that their work came to nothing. Of special interest, however, is the peace offer made by the committee from the association (the Landmarkers, as they were soon to be known), set forth in six propositions, and fairly bristling with the language of an ultimatum:

1. The scriptural right of individual churches to commission and send forth missionaries must be recognized.

2. . . . the reports of missionaries shall include only the work actually performed by the missionaries and paid for by missionary contributers.

3. The recognition of each church as a unit and entitled to equal representation with any other church in Association or Convention.

4. The absolute abolition of the office and expense of the corresponding secretary under whatever title.

5. The right of the churches to instruct their messengers on any subject to be recognized.

6. The abolition of the present plan of co-operation with the Home and Foreign Mission Boards of the Southern Baptist Convention.[10]

[9] *Minutes, Arkansas Baptist State Convention*, 1903, pp. 15–27.
[10] *Ibid.*, p. 16.

The committee from the convention, after complaining about these propositions one by one, agreed to every one of them and brought a report to the convention, meeting at Little Rock in 1903, recommending their adoption in the interests of peace. One man, T. W. O'Kelley, presented a minority report and urged the rejection of the peace terms. The convention, though weak from the defection, was united, and the minority report was adopted. This action marked the final break between the association and the convention, as it has continued for more than fifty years.

Two of the above proposals, the third and the fifth, offer material for a lengthy discussion on Baptist polity. They are based on the assumption that the associations and conventions are composed, not of individuals, but of churches, and therefore these two propositions would logically follow. Leaving aside the question of whether a Baptist church can ever "belong" to any other body—whether it can thus relinquish its sovereignty—one still must deal with the apparent contradiction of this contention with the usual Landmark insistence upon the local church as the only scriptural ecclesiastical body. The acceptance of these articles, of course, would have the further effect of subjecting the association to the control and authority of the churches through the instructions given to messengers; it could not be an independent body within its own sphere of action.

In the Constitution and Statement of Principles of the Baptist General Association, a Landmark organization formed in Texarkana in 1905, may be found a good illustration of the distance which soon separated the convention Baptists and the followers of the Landmark movement:

Article IV. This association when assembled shall be composed of messengers elected by churches in sympathy with its doctrine, purposes and work, and of such messengers only. Each church may elect three messengers.

Article V. Definition. By a Baptist church in this document is meant such a Baptist church as avowedly and distinctly teaches, among other Bible tenets, the following: the essential diety of Jesus Christ; the full inspiration and authority of the Bible as the written word of God . . . the necessity of spiritual regeneration; salvation by grace . . . scriptural baptism and membership in a Baptist church as orderly and essential prerequisites to communion at the Lord's Supper as observed among Baptists.[11]

This is the quiet and formal way of stating the conviction, by this time becoming prevalent among the Landmark people, that they and they alone were maintaining the purity of the gospel. The claims were elsewhere expressed in less restrained language. Witness an article in the *Arkansas Baptist*, a paper owned and published by W. A. Clark, one of the leading Landmarkers of his day:

Why, it is patent as the day that the only true churches of Jesus Christ in the world today are landmark Baptist churches. For landmark churches are simply New Testament churches living and operating in the present hour.

Landmark Baptists alone have and can give the true church and scriptural baptism. We alone can or do set the Lord's table in its scriptural appointments. We alone have divine authority to missionize the world.[12]

And in the same issue of that paper:

Here are the essential features of our Landmarkism: 1. That only Landmark Baptist Churches have any claim upon Christ as their author and founder.

. . . .

[11] *Arkansas Baptist*, March 17, 1909, p. 2.
[12] *Ibid.*, December 1, 1909, p. 2.

9. That Landmark Baptist Churches alone can establish historical connection with New Testament Churches.[13]

Within the brief time, then, from the division in 1902 to this series of statements in 1909, the center of gravity for the Landmark movement has shifted from mission method to a high-church orthodoxy very similar to that of Graves. The nine points from which two are quoted above follow the same general line of thought. Not one of them makes any distinctive point of doctrine concerning God, man, sin, salvation, Christ, the Bible, the future life, the atonement, or Christian behavior. In a word, "Graves-ism" has become the test of orthodoxy. The ideological osmosis by which this Landmarkism has re-entered the Southern Baptist Convention is the center of interest in the remainder of this study.

The Landmarkism of the Southern Baptist Convention

With the withdrawal of the Landmarkers to form their own separate organization, Landmarkism by no means disappeared from the ranks of the Southern Baptist Convention. It may be seen today in the changes in the nature of the Convention itself, both in fact and in popular opinion; in the virtual identification of the kingdom of God and the visible church (with the necessary elimination of any other meaning of *ecclēsia*); in the insistence upon historical succession of Baptist churches since apostolic days; and in the emphasis of a high-church ecclesiology, as in the discussions of "alien immersion," "open communion," and the validity of certain ordinations. The objection on the part of some Baptists to being classified as Protestants also shows this influence.

W. W. Barnes [14] has shown how the changes in the basis

---

[13] *Ibid.*

[14] *The Southern Baptist Convention: A Study in the Development of Ecclesiology* (Seminary Hill, Texas: W. W. Barnes, 1934), pp. 1, 8, 61.

and source of membership of the Southern Baptist Convention reflect the Landmark influence. From an assemblage of people interested in missions and active in the support of a missionary program, the Convention has developed into an ecclesiastical organization.

Through the years the membership of the churches has come to be considered the membership of the convention. Churches that have no interest and take no part in the work of the convention are considered to have an ecclesiastical relationship to the convention. They are listed as "Southern Baptist Churches" and considered as in some way related to the Southern Baptist Convention.[15]

And since such a term is used with what approaches legal precision, some method must be found for defining what is to be counted such a church. Who else can give such a definition but the Southern Baptist Convention? Would not this body be the final authority for Baptists? The attempt of the Landmark brethren to define a church [16] does not sound as strange as it would have sounded a century ago, since Landmarkism has become an integral part of Baptist thought in the church and the Convention.

This development goes naturally with the wish often expressed by the early Landmarkers, and realized in their own organization, to have a convention or association *composed of churches*.

Under the influence of Landmarkism an early effort was made (1859) to limit the messengers to members of regular Baptist churches. An effort was made in 1869 to limit the representation to churches. Time and again, in some form or another, it was proposed to have only church representation. . . . The associational basis of membership and the specious argument for mag-

[15] *Ibid.*, p. 74.
[16] Cf. ante, footnote 10.

nifying the church tended to bring into the state organization and into the Southern Baptist Convention the view of church representation only. . . . The Landmark idea of general organizations being composed of churches has not yet been incorporated in the constitution of the convention, but it is little short of it and perhaps ultimately will be done.[17]

Graves's identification of the church with the kingdom of God deserves careful attention, for here again his Landmark position is strongly felt in the Southern Baptist Convention fellowship today: "The church and kingdom of Christ is an institution, an organization; he, as God of heaven, 'set it up,' he built it, and it must therefore be visible." [18] When this assertion is coupled with the claim of Baptist churches to exclusive recognition as true churches of Christ, it bears a strong resemblance to the preaching from many pulpits today. From this comes the rejection of any idea of an invisible church or of the church in its worldwide sense.

And this, too, is manifest, that the only church that is revealed to us is a visible church, and the only church with which we have any . . . duties to perform, is a *visible* body. . . . If this is visible, he has no invisible kingdom or church, and such a thing has no real existence in heaven or earth.[19]

Since the two are to be identified, according to the axiom of Graves, it would follow that their definitions must be stated exclusively in terms of each other: the kingdom embraces the churches and nothing else; the churches, nothing else, constitute the kingdom. Thus one cannot enter the kingdom without becoming a member of one of the true churches of Christ.

The distinctive point made by the Landmark position in

[17] Barnes, *op. cit.*, pp. 72–73.
[18] Graves, *Old Landmarkism: What Is It?*, p. 32.
[19] *Ibid.*

the matter of church succession is not the mere belief in
the existence of such a succession but the insistence upon
its necessity. Where historical documentation cannot provide
a link with the Cathari, Paulicians, Bogomils, Montanists,
Henricians, and others, the gap is usually filled by the quotation of the promise expressed in Matthew 16:18 ff. But here
a serious problem presents itself. If the local church is the
only church and the word *ecclēsia* is not to be used in any
other sense except figuratively,[20] then of course the promise
of perpetuity was made to a local church, that in Jerusalem,
and the promise seems to have been nullified in the days of
Bar-Cochba. And the insistence upon succession as essential
for valid baptism demands that a break in the chain be regarded with equal seriousness, whether the critical date be
A.D. 1941, 1641, or 441. In the Southern Baptist Convention
there is evidence of increasing tension over this and related
problems, tension which manifests itself in proposed or
actual legislation on matters of church recognition, acceptance
of alien immersion as valid baptism, and affiliations of local
churches.

This has led to a decrease in the emphasis given to the
autonomy of the local church. While the church is the final
authority on earth in matters pertaining to its own work,
at least in theory, the associations or conventions may be
developing into superior ecclesiastical bodies which have the
power to define the rights of that otherwise autonomous
body, the local church, and to discipline it in cases of violation of convention decree.

A classic example of this may be seen in an action of the
Arkansas Baptist State Convention in 1949, when a proposed amendment to the constitution was offered to expand
the statement on a "regular Baptist church" into a definition

[20] *Ibid.*, p. 39.

by limitation in four areas. The amendment could not be adopted in this meeting because of the constitutional procedure for approving such amendments, but it was referred to a committee for study and a report the following year. Later in the 1949 meeting, however, a resolution deploring the same practices which would have been forbidden by the proposed amendment was presented and adopted. The amendment was never adopted, and the resolution had no more effect than resolutions usually have, but the episode served one purpose. It said that in the eyes of the messengers of that year, at least, the Arkansas Baptist State Convention is an ecclesiastical body, capable of formulating doctrinal statements and of enforcing them, if need be, with exclusion from the body.

It is just at this point that the struggle between the historic Baptist position and the doctrine of Landmarkism is likely to be concentrated for at least another decade. Out of its resolution will emerge the general pattern for the Baptist doctrine of the church and the future course of the Southern Baptist Convention, perhaps for generations to come. The impulses set in motion by J. R. Graves in the Baptist family have not yet spent their force, and their final and total effects remain to be seen.

IX

AN INTERPRETATION OF CHRISTIAN STEWARDSHIP

Paul Leonard Stagg

The discussion of stewardship often proceeds in an atmosphere of legalism rather than of grace. Such a point of view is mistaken from the standpoint of Christian theology and leads to a distorted conception of biblical stewardship. The distortion is apparent in various ways—the meeting of a rule is put above the meeting of a need, duty is put above grateful response, external action is stressed more than inner motive, mathematical calculation overshadows the spontaneity of love in giving without measure, the bondage of the law takes the place of the freedom of the Spirit, and fragmentary giving—money but not self, a fixed part of one's money but not the responsible use of all—takes the place of wholeness in giving.

From the biblical point of view stewardship is grateful and obedient response to God for his undeserved gifts, acknowledging him as the ultimate owner and sovereign Lord of life, which is held by man as a trust, issuing in the voluntary and responsible use of one's total self and possessions to the glory of God and in loving service to one's neighbor.

The Motive of Christian Stewardship

In the Bible, as in life itself, the motives of stewardship are often mixed and run the gamut from a shrewd bargain

with God, a *quid pro quo* by which his favor is sought, to
a grateful response of self-giving in remembrance of God's
redemptive acts. Between these contrasting motivations in
giving is a tremendous difference which colors the whole
quality of living. In the one case, religion is a bargain which
one strikes with God, something which one does to *earn*
his favor and reward. In the other case, religion is not an
attempt to win the favor of God but a thankful acknowledgment for gifts already received which themselves evoke man's
gift of life and substance. In the former case, there is a
strained quality to giving; in the latter case, giving is a gracious
act.

At the lowest level, in the earliest times as well as in later
forms, the gift offering was a bargaining instrument, very
largely a bribe in nature. When Jacob made a vow to God,
the condition was that he would give a gift to God in exchange
for God's presence, protection, and material provision. "Jacob
vowed a vow, saying, If God will be with me, and will keep
me in this way that I go, and will give me bread to eat,
and raiment to put on, so that I come again to my father's
house in peace; then shall the Lord be my God . . . and of
all that thou shalt give me I will surely give the tenth unto
thee" (Gen. 28:20–22). The bargain here is that Jacob will
give a gift in return for something. This kind of gift stands
in sharp contrast to true Christian giving, which is based on
a wholly different understanding of God's nature, namely,
that God is a gracious God who gives his gifts freely, not as
the result of a bargain, and bestows them upon his unde-
serving children. Christian giving is prompted by a gift already given, not to earn something but to express gratitude.

Related to the bargaining idea in making gifts is the idea
of giving gifts to God as a tribute. Just as the earthly land-
owner demanded dues for the use of his lands, so some be-

lieved that God required a tribute. The tribute idea was related to the bargain idea because the gifts given to Yahweh were often regarded as an inducement to him, as the bestower of fertility to soil and beast, to grant his blessings. But the idea of tribute also stood for acknowledgment that "the earth is the Lord's and the fulness thereof," and, as such, its implications for man's stewardship have a universal validity. The exact form and amount of the tribute, in the form of a tax, is not binding upon Christians, but the principle of acknowledgment of God's ownership is binding. Much depends on the way in which this acknowledgment is made, whether as a matter of mere duty and legal requirement or as a matter of faith issuing into gratitude and love.

While the Israelite often regarded his gift as a bargaining instrument, it would be false to assume that there was never a disinterested gift stemming from gratitude. The truth is that the sense of gratitude is innate in man; and often, after having received some gift, the impulse to recognize the gift prompted an offering of thanksgiving. In his study of the agricultural period of Israel's history, Oesterley has cited a number of examples to show that the thank offerings seem to have been illustrations of disinterested gratitude. Among the illustrations cited is Jacob's offering of thanksgiving for his safe journey to Beersheba (Gen. 46:1).[1] There were also offerings to do homage to God, freewill offerings, purely voluntary gifts offered to God, such as gifts for the tabernacle furniture (Ex. 35:29; 36:3) and for the Temple (2 Chron. 31:14; Ezra 1:6; 8:28).

Many writers present stewardship in terms of the Old Testament tithe and thus become involved in a legalism that misses the deeper motivation of the Old Testament, with its

---

[1] Cf. W. O. E. Oesterley, *Sacrifices in Ancient Israel* (London: Hodder and Stoughton, 1937), p. 133.

emphasis upon grateful obedience to God for his deliverance of Israel.

The book of Deuteronomy bases the faith of Israel squarely upon the completely unmerited love of God made known in his deliverance of the Hebrew people from bondage, his guidance in the wilderness, and his gift of land to them. The theological setting of the law within grace is thus dramatically fixed. The God who loves Israel evokes from his people the response of gratitude—willing and glad obedience to his will in all of life. Standing over all laws is the well-beloved Shema (Deut. 6:4–5), enjoining love for God, complete devotion of one's whole being in glad response for God's unmerited love. To put it in New Testament terms, "We love, because he first loved us" (1 John 4:19, RSV).

The Tithe and Christian Stewardship

The tithe is widely commended as the minimum requirement of Christian giving. While much may be said for adopting the tithe voluntarily as a standard for one's giving without rigidly imposing it upon others as a Christian requirement, it is clear in adopting such a practice that one is not carrying on the Old Testament practice. At most one is doing something only remotely analogous to the tithing practice of the Old Testament, which was a tax to support the Temple and the priestly system, a social and religious system which no longer exists.[2] Tithes were obligatory in Judaism as a tax until the destruction of the Temple in A.D. 70, but they are not thus binding upon Christians.

The emphasis upon the third-year tithe being kept in the offerer's own city for relief of the poor is in sharp contrast to the position of Christian legalists who insist, reading Malachi

[2] An insight from a letter to the author by Lawrence E. Toombs, assistant professor of Old Testament at Drew University.

out of context, that the whole tithe must be brought to the storehouse, which is interpreted as the church as the successor of the Temple. In this respect Christian legalists are more rigorous than the Old Testament, for the Old Testament provided that the tithe might be used for benevolences through other channels than the Temple. This is not to detract from the need of adequate support for the church, nor from the desirability of tithing in voluntary support of it, but it is to indicate the dubious grounds on which legalists stand when they claim that the Christian is required to give his whole tithe to the church under *every* circumstance and that in so doing he is adhering to the *Old Testament* view of the tithe.

In resolving the question of the tithe's applicability to Christians, the New Testament is decisive. The tithe as a legalistic requirement is alien to the whole tenor of Paul's teachings, and while there is no reason for believing that Jesus did not approve the tithe as a support for the Temple cultus, there is no evidence that he would have enforced it upon Christians as a legal requirement. The statement in Matthew 23:23, "Ye tithe mint and anise and cummin, and have left undone the weightier matters of the law, justice, and mercy, and faith: but these ye ought to have done, and not to have left the other undone" (ASV), is often cited in proof that Jesus taught Christians to tithe as a minimum requirement. This is dubious exegesis which violates the context and misses the point of the verse. The context shows that the saying was a stricture upon the Pharisees and scribes, and its application is to them, not to Christians, who ought not to be lumped indiscriminately with Pharisees! The point here is that the scribes and Pharisees by their emphasis upon the legalistic requirements of the oral tradition had missed the deeper meaning of the Torah, which is a revelation of God's love, justice, and mercy. They thus confused the trivial with the important, the less with the greater, the ceremonial with the moral, and put all things on the same footing. The enduring principle for Christians is that they must not allow adherence to rigid rules to keep them from attending to weightier matters.

Since the Gospels themselves give a variety of statements concerning the relationship of Jesus to the law, ranging from complete rejection of the law to its complete affirmation,[3] it is not strange that scholars differ among themselves as to the precise relationship of Jesus to the law. There is consensus, however, that Jesus did not countenance code morality. Between Jesus and the scribes and Pharisees there was a fixed gulf. For Jesus, righteous living was the spontaneous expression of a transformed life; for the scribes and Pharisees, it was obedience to a code, an external discipline imposed from without. The corollary of this, as T. W. Manson has well expressed it, is "that it is a mistake to regard the ethical teaching of Jesus as a 'New Law' in the sense of a reformed and simplified exposition of the Old, or as a code of rules to take the place of the code of Moses and his successors."[4] Instead of offering a set of rules of conduct, Jesus gave a number of illustrations of the way a transformed character would express itself in action. In fulfilling one's stewardship to a neighbor beaten by robbers there is no neat, mechanical, or mathematical rule to satisfy. Love, moved by a neighbor's need, is prompted to satisfy it at whatever risk or cost to self.

When Jesus discussed the two great commandments (Luke 10:25–37; Mark 12:29–31), he revealed a clean break with all legalism. Love cannot be coerced or legislated or made

[3] Cf. B. H. Branscomb, *Jesus and the Law of Moses* (New York: R. R. Smith, Inc., 1930), pp. 2 ff.

[4] T. W. Manson, *The Teaching of Jesus* (Cambridge: The University Press, 1951), p. 301.

to fit rules of conduct or stewardship. For this reason the two great commandments do not prescribe or forbid any particular action but assume that a transformed character will express itself in the light of the needs of one's neighbor.

Paul, who considered Christ as the end of the law and wrote Galatians as a charter of Christian freedom, could hardly be expected to give the tithe any place in his thought as a legal requirement. This assumption is borne out in his writings. Nowhere did he enjoin the tithe upon Christians, least of all in the place where it would most likely occur if it had occupied any place in his thinking, his appeal for a collection for the saints of Jerusalem. In 1 Corinthians 16:1 ff. and 2 Corinthians 8 and 9, the apostle appealed for proportionate giving as one might prosper, but he suggested no fixed percentage of income. The collection was not exacted but elicited as a voluntary, "cheerful" gift. While he appealed to other motives—reciprocity, the example of other Christians, and the need of the Jerusalem Christians—he nowhere mentioned the tithe. The basic appeal for generous giving was the sacrificial example of Jesus Christ. Paul clearly expected Christian stewardship to be discharged, not in conformity to a rule but as a grateful response to "the grace of our Lord Jesus Christ." As such it would not be "grudging, or of necessity" (2 Cor. 9:7) but freehearted and generous, "for God loveth a cheerful giver." While such love is not bound by rules, it is not directionless but, rather, unconditionally bound to one's neighbor; and "the needs of other persons are the rule of love and quickly teach such love what to do." [5] What should be done in a particular circumstance is not known in advance from some code but is discovered by Christian love from what it apprehends to be the needs of others.

[5] Paul Ramsey, *Basic Christian Ethics* (New York: Charles Scribner's Sons, 1952), p. 66.

Tithing in the Early Church

While tithing is taken for granted by many today as binding upon Christians and not simply as a desirable system when voluntarily accepted, in the early Christian church tithing was not resorted to for several centuries. Little was heard of it until the fourth century. As the church spread and an ecclesiastical establishment was built up, it fell back upon rule, based upon the legal provision of the tithe, and the Christian priest was regarded as analogous to the Jewish priest and Levite. However, while the Council of Macon (A.D. 585) ordained payment of tithes and provided for the excommunication of those who refused to pay, the tithe was not adopted without opposition, many, like Epiphanius, holding that the tithe was no more binding for Christians than circumcision.[6]

These facts do not make it necessary to reject tithing as a method of giving, which may be desirable enough when undertaken voluntarily. The need is to avoid tithing as a legal system and as a substitute for the kind of stewardship prompted by "faith working through love" and geared to the needs of one's neighbor, which the New Testament sanctions. If a Christian practices tithing, he should be careful to avoid the pretension that there is special merit in the sight of God in making his gifts in this particular way. Moreover, he should avoid the legalism of rigidly insisting that the practice must be carried out irrespective of special circumstances and situations. Finally, he must be careful to avoid the kind of casuistry, practiced in the Old Testament, which claims the credit for tithing while exempting some things from the tithe by dubious devices.

[6] Cf. "Tithing" in James Hastings, *Encyclopedia of Religion and Ethics* (Edinburgh: T. & T. Clark; New York: Charles Scribner's Sons, 1908–26).

While tithing has manifold values—gives a definite plan, puts the church first in giving, lifts giving from haphazard, token gifts, and reminds Christians of the wider meaning of stewardship—its limitations ought to be clearly seen. It is apt to stress giving to meet a rule instead of a need.

Stewardship of Possessions

A caution as to the meaning of stewardship must here be observed. There is a popular misconception that God has ordained that some shall have property and others not and that those who have it are stewards on behalf of those who do not. On several scores this is untenable theologically. Nowhere does the Bible assert that God intends some to have wealth and others to depend upon them. Such a concept assumes that the social stratification between the privileged and the downtrodden is ordained of God and leaves out of account the element of human sin in the disproportion between the strong and the weak. By sanctifying a social stratification, in part due to man's greed and will-to-power, it thus adds insult to injury. This is not a plea for a flat equalitarianism, which rules out difference, but rather for a rejection of a dubious concept of stewardship which seems to sanctify an inordinate disproportion between the wealthy and the poor by saying that God has made the wealthy to be stewards in behalf of the poor. Such a view usually issues in a show of philanthropy, a completely inadequate charity, which sprays an aroma of paternalism over the cesspool of man's injustice to man. Philanthropy has its place as a legitimate expression of stewardship but never as a means of perpetuating injustice by becoming a sop to conscience and a pallid substitute for a dynamic change of the political, social, and economic structure responsible for the injustice.

Jesus had deep convictions with respect to the use of riches which are important for a doctrine of stewardship. The following summary [7] of his teaching is crucial:

Jesus ruled out the worship of material things by affirming that one must put God and his kingdom first. Along with the Old Testament, he saw possessions as good—as means, never as the end of life. Seeing how men accumulated things, hoarded them, covetously desired them, Jesus knew their peril, how they could come to take the place of God. So he said, "Ye cannot serve God and mammon." Mammon, the Aramaic word for riches, was the object of worship of many people, and Jesus warned that it was almost impossible for a rich man to enter the kingdom of God (Mark 10:23–27). Yet the peril was not only in the possession of wealth but also in the coveting of wealth by which, for the poor also, mammon was made god. The principle for stewardship is that material possession must not become the end of existence, as a rival for God's place, but must be used to enrich life.

A second principle laid down by Jesus is that persons are more valuable than possessions, that love for the kingdom of God means love for man and the refusal to sacrifice personal values for material values. A man could lose his soul by putting money above the claims of person. As an example of the radical therapy needed by one individual, and as an indication of the primacy of persons over wealth, Jesus bade a rich young ruler sell all that he had and give to the poor (Matt. 19:21). A rich man who built larger barns to house his bumper crops, while the poor were neglected about him, came under the judgment of God. In his sin of worshiping things he had reversed the order of values; he put money above men.

Another principle enunicated by Jesus is that one's vocation

[7] Cf. B. H. Branscomb's excellent discussion in *The Teachings of Jesus* (Nashville: Cokesbury Press, 1931), pp. 217 ff.

should be motivated by the desire to serve, not solely for personal profit. To be sure, there is nothing in the teachings of Jesus which would rule out the profit incentive in production, but there is much which would bring it under responsible control and which would relate it to service and the needs of one's neighbor. The teaching of Jesus here is clear and emphatic: He who would become the greatest must become the minister of all (Mark 10:44; Matt. 20:27; Luke 9:48).

Production solely for profit is both poor economics and poor Christianity—poor economics because it leaves unsolved the problem of distribution and poor Christianity because it makes money the end of life and fails to see how it must serve the needs of man. How often preaching has emphasized the need of tithing and has left unexamined and unchallenged the motive of production conceived solely in terms of profit!

In the discharge of stewardship Jesus was not so much impressed by size and quantity as he was by the motive, quality, and faithfulness of the giver and the gift. Is not taking bigness as the measure that counts, whether in business or church, a far cry from that kind of stewardship Jesus praised when "a poor widow came, and put in two copper coins, which make a penny"? It was not the amount alone that impressed Jesus but the faithfulness of the act: "For they all contributed out of their abundance; but she out of her poverty has put in everything she had, her whole living" (Mark 12:44, RSV).

Christian Stewardship and Rewards

There is often a subtle, sidelong glance at possible rewards for faithful stewardship. Presentations of stewardship may even make a crass appeal to self-interest. While there is enough connection between righteousness and prosperity to give some credence to prudential morality, there is serious criticism to be raised.

The most obvious criticism is the well-known discrepancy between the theory and the fact. While the theory calls for righteousness to be rewarded and evil to be punished, the fact is often enough the opposite to trouble men like Job whose experiences of adversity could not be made to fit a neat formula. The thrust of Job is that spirituality can ultimately neither be motivated nor justified by the reward of prosperity. Spirituality can be sustained despite adversity and brings a reward, which is not so much sought as added and which transcends materialism.

A second criticism is that stewardship for rewards makes salvation depend on the "righteousness of work," a reward which man earns by his fidelity. It shifts the motivation of stewardship from grateful response to God for gifts already received to a self-seeking attempt to earn his gifts. The right approach seems rather to be that in gratitude to God Christians give themselves in responsible stewardship; as a surprise, rewards come which no one has reason to expect.

This suggests a final criticism concerning rewards as a motivation of stewardship. While reward may strengthen Christian action and indicate that the universe is not neutral or capriciously perverse, reward is never the goal of Christian action. As Ramsey has cogently put it:

Reward is always *added* to the nature of the act, not a direct result of it such as might become a part of the agent's own prudential calculation. If he were calculating, the nature of his act would change, it would not be the kind of action for which a reward is promised. If he acts *for the sake of* reward, he has not yet done what God requires of him in readiness for the kingdom, he has not yet become entirely trusting and obedient, not yet single-minded in obedient love.[8]

[8] Ramsey, *op. cit.*, p. 133 f.

Despite this criticism the protest may be entered that
Jesus offered material rewards to his disciples. It is true
that men were urged to seek the kingdom of God and promised that "all these things" should be added to them (Matt.
6:33), that men were to humble themselves that they might
be exalted (Matt. 23:12), and that they were to forsake friends
and possessions and thereby receive them back a hundredfold.
While these sayings must be taken in context and in the light of
Jesus' total teaching, it must be squarely admitted that the
thought of reward in Jesus' teachings is very prominent.
Actually, Jesus never thought of reward in any crude, literal,
materialistic sense. This is evident from many sayings which
condemn action springing from bargaining motives; for example, "Do good, and lend, expecting nothing in return"
(Luke 6:35, RSV), may be taken as a watchword of all his
teachings.

As the Gospels make abundantly clear, Jesus criticized self-
seeking righteousness. In his conflict with the Pharisees, he
criticized in scathing language good deeds done from a selfish
motive, whether charity to the poor or prayer in the mar-
ketplace. Persons with a shrewd eye for a reward for their
good deeds and a desire to be seen of men had their reward
(Matt. 6:2, 5).

Since Jesus' teachings on rewards seem at first glance to be
in conflict with his emphasis on love as the motive of action,
understanding them requires a perspective based on reading
them in their contexts. For one thing, Jesus thought of reward
only in terms of a gift from God, never from man. It was
God's approval one was to seek, not man's. Seeking only
God's reward would eliminate all the selfishness and in-
sincerity that accompany working for reward from men. If
one were seeking man's recompense, he could fool his fellow
man; but the God "who sees in secret" and who knows one's

inmost intent could not be deceived. Working for God's reward simply means, as Branscomb has put it, "trusting God that unselfish service to our fellow men will result in the highest and best in life for ourselves." [9]

When Jesus spoke of working for reward, he was really giving the assurance that one's trust in God was not misplaced; for God would be waiting to bestow his blessings far beyond one's deserving. This kind of righteousness is far removed from "work righteousness." As Branscomb has said,

From his teaching on the reward of goodness, the insincere motive is gone, and the self-righteousness of the Pharisee is gone, and humility and gratitude and joy take their place. When one sees the character of God that Jesus revealed, the motive for doing good becomes grateful love rather than a desire to earn a reward. There is a vast difference between this and a selfish morality.[10]

For another thing, putting Jesus' teaching on reward in perspective shows that material wealth is not the blessing God is eager to bestow upon the faithful steward. The sayings of Jesus make it clear that wealth is not always to be regarded as a blessing—a truth shown in such warnings as "Lay not up for yourselves treasures upon earth" (Matt. 6:19), or "It is easier for a camel to go through the eye of a needle, than for a rich man to enter into the kingdom of God (Mark 10:25). Moreover, apart from the perils attending possessions, Jesus emphasized that the greatest blessings do not lie in possessions but in the fuller and richer life of service in the kingdom of God. "What does it profit a man," he asked, "if a man gain the whole world and miss the kingdom?" He was evidently thinking of "true riches" (Luke 16:11), which cannot be equated with "unrighteous mammon."

[9] Branscomb, *The Teachings of Jesus,* p. 249.
[10] *Ibid.,* p. 251.

When the verses which are cited to prove that Jesus taught a material reward for faithful service are examined in their own context, they reveal another meaning. Matthew 6:33, often cited to prove that prosperity will follow faithful stewardship, is a promise only of food and clothing and not great wealth. The faithful who forsake all for Jesus' cause (Mark 10:29 f.) may receive a hundredfold in return, but such words as "houses" and "mothers" cannot be taken literally. No man can receive a hundred mothers. The words "with persecution" indicate that the early disciples did not expect their fidelity to be rewarded by comfort and exemption from privation. Each of the Beatitudes promises a reward, but the reward of the pure of heart is not a flourishing business but a vision of God, and, it may be added, only the pure of heart would regard the vision of God as a reward. The Son of man who had nowhere "to lay his head" and who, at length, was crucified could hardly be expected to offer his followers earthly prosperity and security.

The reward for fidelity to Christ is life itself, eternal life in his kingdom. This is not gained by human merit but as a gift beyond the deserving even of a faithful steward. As the parable of the laborers in the vineyard makes clear, when believers have done all the things commanded them, they are still "unprofitable servants." While God will take care of his own, even as he has regard for a sparrow, he gives no guarantee of earthly wealth or safety. As a faithful steward, one may have to give up wealth if it stands in the way of love for Christ, or forsake family and kindred for his cause, or "lose" one's life in his service.

Christian giving must always be kept on a high level and not cheapened in a spurious attempt to increase gifts to the "budget" by appeal to mercenary reward. Yet how often either the need for funds for the church or the desire for prosperity as the price of one's piety has prompted such base appeal.

Until there is a wholly different point of view, biblically based and soundly theological, there can be little hope of substantial improvement in the stewardship of life and substance. Preaching duty may "get results" of a certain sort, even raise the budget, but preaching duty never makes great Christians. There is a fixed gulf between a calculating stewardship that obeys mechanical rules and fixed proportions and often, in however refined a way, seeks to bribe God by making a token payment and, on the other hand, a stewardship that yields glad obedience to God for his undeserved gifts and seeks to use responsibly the whole of life for his glory and the good of one's neighbor. No one can catch the full significance of this biblical view and put it in a single stewardship tract or sermon. It is a message which must subtly pervade every sermon and tract until life is freed from its strained quality and the spontaneity of life is restored.

X

DISCIPLINE IN THE CHURCH

Theron D. Price

THE CHURCH is called to share in and to show forth the holiness of her Lord. In the Bible this call to holiness is addressed to the whole congregation and is not concerned merely with the church's holy rites or ordained leadership. That is to say, with S. L. Greenslade, that the church's call to be holy "involves the consecration and actual sanctification of its individual members."

At the same time, the church's gospel is good news precisely for sinners. The church declares through this gospel that God in Christ has redeemed the race by slaying its mortal enemies —sin, death, hell. It thus calls on men—weak, sinful, and foolish as they are—to enter into their proper heritage as the family of God. This is to say, on the other hand, that the church's members while yet imperfect are promised both forgiveness of sins and "moral and spiritual growth within the fellowship of the Church." [1]

The three principal concerns of the church, as touching on the integrity of her own life, are the purity of her doctrine, the holiness of her members, and the unity of her fellowship. This requires, of course, that the church look on nothing with greater apprehension than impurity of teaching (heresy), moral and spiritual lapse (sin), and breach of fellowship (schism).

[1] S. L. Greenslade, *Schism in the Early Church* (New York: Harper & Brothers, 1950), p. 10.

164

To all these dangers the church addresses her *discipline*. In the widest sense discipline includes, positively, the nurture of sound doctrine, sound character, and sound unity as well as, negatively, remedial correction for heresy, sin, and schism. The positive side includes the church's program of education and the formulation of her confessions of faith. The negative includes censures of one sort or another which put the offense and guilt of a member under ban. This twofold connotation of the word *discipline* explains why—in early Baptist circles, for example—"confessions of faith" and "abstracts of discipline" were usually published in a single volume.

This chapter shall deal, not with the (positive) task of maintaining the spiritual purity of the Christian community and of preventing sin and error through healthy teaching, but rather with the (negative) task of correcting heresy, moral lapse, and schism once they have appeared and begun to impair or destroy the church's life. Because Christians, too, are subject to the limitations and frailties of humanity, these "occasions of scandal" do come. Because the church is by nature the fellowship of the Holy Spirit, the character of her discipline must be purely spiritual.[2] Materials for study will be drawn from the New Testament and other early Christian literature and from books of discipline published by Baptist associations.

Discipline in the Early Church

The most important New Testament passage on discipline would appear to be Matthew 18:15–18, given as Jesus' own words:

If your brother sins against you, go and tell him his fault, between you and him alone. If he listens to you, you have gained

[2] Cf. *New Schaff-Herzog Encyclopedia of Religious Knowledge* (Grand Rapids: Baker Book House, 1949–1950), III, 86.

your brother. But if he does not listen, take one or two others along with you, that every word may be confirmed by the evidence of two or three witnesses. If he refuses to listen to them, tell it to the church; and if he refuses to listen even to the church, let him be to you as a Gentile and a tax collector. Truly, I say to you, whatever you bind on earth shall be bound in heaven, and whatever you loose on earth shall be loosed in heaven (RSV).

The practical application of this sort of teaching in the apostolic church appears in 1 Corinthians 5 and 2 Corinthians 2:4–8. The first of these two passages concerns fornication in the church, which the congregation was tolerating. In words that imply formal excommunication, Paul called upon the church "to deliver this man to Satan for the destruction of the flesh, that his spirit may be saved in the day of the Lord Jesus" (v. 5, RSV). That these words produced the desired effect on the congregation would seem to be indicated in the second passage (2 Cor. 2:4–8) where the apostle recommended forgiveness and comfort for the offender.

From these verses emerge several items of note:

(1) The recommended discipline was grounded in love. Paul's love of the congregation produced a severe attitude toward that which threatened them—sin (v. 4). The attitude was not an expression of private opinion but of moral judgment (v. 5). (2) Discipline was not mechanically applied but in measure and means suitable to the reclamation of the offender (v. 6a). This was not penance in the medieval sense, by which one could atone for his wrong. The discipline aimed rather at the reclamation of the offender (v. 7). (3) Reclamation being effected, positive fellowship with the offender was to be confirmed in *agapē*. There must be no continuing suspicions and no spirit of retaliation (v. 8). (4) It was the congregation which exercised this discipline. There

were no professional officers who had this duty (v. 6b).

It seems fair to say that these passages indicate the spirit and procedure of true disciplinary action. The problem in Corinth had to do with gross and public sin. Other situations also called for ecclesiastical rebuke for the sake of protecting the church's integrity and of reclaiming the offender. The pastoral epistles, for example, contain advice as to how to deal with unsound teaching and factious actions.[3]

From the passages listed thus far the following appears to be established: The occasions for discipline are *sin* and *error*. Sin may appear either as moral lapse or as factious spirit—eating into the congregation's health like a canker and putting the church to open shame. Error takes any form of unsound doctrine. It subverts souls and undermines the church's witness.

The experience of the church in the second century throws abundant light on these matters. In general, the church became more rigoristic in the second century than it had been in the first. It is well to note, however, that the second-century rigorism reveals more than a strong sense of moral responsibility. It involves as well a partial reinterpretation of sin and a sizeable reorientation of the idea of faith.

The *Didache*, a small treatise of prime importance for the study of second-century congregational life, represents the church as a community of mutual fellowship and mutual rebuke. One is instructed not only in how to baptize or conduct the Lord's Supper but also in how to test prophets (xiii, xiv). Fellowship is withdrawn from one who has wronged a neighbor (xv. 3), and the whole life of believers is to be regulated by the gospel of the Lord (xv. 4).[4]

[3] Cf. 2 Tim. 2:17; Titus 3:10; 2 John 10–11.

[4] For an estimate of the place of the *Didache* in postapostolic Christianity see E. J. Goodspeed, *A History of Early Christian Literature* (Chicago: The University of Chicago Press, 1942), p. 158 f.

The larger evidence on discipline comes in connection with sins of a public nature, which exposed the church to open shame. On this type of problem there is considerable elaboration of policy. For this, *The Shepherd* by Hermas serves as the amplest second-century document.

The Shepherd, which gives a vivid picture of early second-century Christianity in Rome, deals principally with the theme of repentance and specifically with the problem of the possibility of repentance for sins committed after baptism. Hermas affirms that sin after baptism may be forgiven only one time, but this is not as significant as the fact that his whole exposition rests on a serious misunderstanding, both as to sin's nature and its cure.[5] Sin, as the very principle of self-assertion in the face of the divine sovereignty and will to fellowship becomes, for Hermas, a series of sinful acts viewed as formal shortcomings in the face of external demands. Hermas' understanding both of sin and of repentance is quite legalistic. It contributes materially to the later Roman Catholic doctrine of penance. Of a piece with this is Hermas' hint—the first in Christian literature—of the idea of supererogation. While the word is not used, the idea is clear that one can, by works of love, more than fulfil the requirements of law and righteousness and so obtain a special reward.

These illustrations from the *Didache* and *The Shepherd* serve to show the development of a new concept of sin. It comes to be construed as the sum total of sins. Its meaning is legalized and its remission mechanized. The church's discipline, therefore, was being built on flimsier theological foundations than were actually available. Discipline apart from right theological foundations is always both inadequate and dangerous. Hermas has classed three sins as unforgivable by the church. These three, later to be extended to seven

[5] Cf. Vision III, Similitude IX, Commandment IV, and Similitude VIII.

and called *mortal* sins, were adultery, idolatry or apostasy, and murder. In actual practice, however, the church began to make special dispensation even for these.[6]

In the disciplinary action of the church, sin was not the only concern. Heresy, too, posed a serious problem. The word "heresy" originally meant a view or opinion out of harmony with the norm by which it was measured. In early Christian literature it means as much "schism" as "heresy" as the latter is currently used. By the third century the fathers were applying the term to any serious deviation from the faith.[7]

Though the idea of heresy as undermining the apostolic tradition may be germinally present in the pastoral epistles, it is the epistles of Ignatius (*ca.* A.D. 110) [8] that first contain the notion that heretics are family corrupters and that heresy will damn souls.

It is not the purpose here to give a theological estimate of heresy and the problem which it poses for the church in history. One must remark, however, that any estimate of the problem of heresy of necessity reflects one's understanding of that "faith" from which the "heresy" is a deviation. In this connection it must be said that, at least, the Pauline concept of faith undergoes a reorientation beginning by the early second century.

Paul's use of "faith" carries the force of total personal commitment to the will and way of God. It involves the recognition on man's part of his complete unworthiness, his spiritual

[6] The first bishop recorded as readmitting a sexual offender to the church's communion was Callistus, Bishop of Rome, A.D. 217–222. The readmittance of apostatizers came during the episcopate of Cornelius of Rome, A.D. 251–253. The decision to readmit to communion persons guilty of bloodshed cannot be so specifically documented, but was operative by at least the early sixth century.

[7] Cf. Schaff-Herzog, *op. cit.*, V, 234.

[8] *Epistle to the Ephesians* 16:1; 17:1; cf. *Epistle to the Trallians*, 9.

bankruptcy, his absolute inability to achieve the ends of life. Such recognition of total need issues in total trust in God to provide as sheer gift what man could not earn as just desert. There seems to be in the Pauline letters no element of "correct doctrine" in the meaning of "faith." In Ignatius there is included precisely this element of "right belief," or "correct doctrine," and this represents a change in Christian thought which is not for the better.[9]

Still a further point requires notice, the locus of responsibility for the administration of discipline. This responsibility was originally committed to the congregation. This is due to the fact, which Karl Barth has pointed out,[10] that the church was and properly is "the living congregation of the living Lord Jesus Christ." It is only within the living fellowship of Redeemer with redeemed that sin, heresy, and schism can be understood. For the essence of the church is not found in orthodox confessions, ordained clergy, or venerable rites and institutions. The church is the body of Christ, the living fellowship of believers under the word and Spirit of God. Indeed, Professor Barth, in a manner highly suggestive if perhaps extreme, defines the church as an event (*Ereignis*) in which the life and fellowship of the community of faith is constantly being created and renewed by the living Lord through the Holy Spirit. The one government which guarantees the unity and protects the integrity of this living congregation is the concern alone of the living Lord and of his Word.

Due to the pressure of circumstances and the currents of powerful theological forces, the government of the church increasingly centered in the clergy, and the administration of

[9] Cf. *Ephesians* 7:2; 9:1, and the whole temper of chapters 16–20.
[10] World Council of Churches, *Man's Disorder and God's Design* (New York: Harper & Brothers, 1949), I, 67 ff.

discipline became one of the distinctive clerical responsibilities. This takes added significance when it is recalled that, with the problems posed by divisive movements in the second century and with the increase of disciplinary problems occasioned by lapse during persecution in the third century, the church cultivated more a "pastoral" than a "prophetic" policy. The disciplinary rigor of the second century declined somewhat in the third. Excommunication from the fellowship of the church continued for centuries to be the chief form of extreme disciplinary action. A chief problem in its application was to administer it in such way that from its use one could hope both to protect the church's integrity and to reclaim the offender.

In summary of what has thus far been said, the following points appear: (1) The *occasion* for discipline was heresy, sin, or schism. (2) The church, acting directly or through its leaders, was the *agent* of disciplinary action. (3) The true *spirit* of discipline was love rather than retaliation. (4) The *aims* of discipline were the protection of the church and reclamation of the offender. (5) The *practice* of discipline reflected the community's current views of sin, faith, and the nature of the church. Such modifications in practice as appeared reflected not only the church's quality of moral sensitivity but, as well, her advance in the legalization of the idea of sin and the mechanization of its forgiveness. (6) The *quality* of the church's discipline can never be separated from her proper concern for sin and her understanding of grace. This quality must be determined by its faithfulness to the mind of Christ and the measure of genuine Christian spirit in the aim and manner of enforcement.

Some of the basic issues in the life of the early church have been brought under review and may serve as illustrations of the broader story. The Roman, Lutheran, and Reformed disciplines, which ought to have fair exposition as parts of the total subject, must here be passed by in order to deal with the discipline of the Baptists.

Discipline in Baptist Churches

The church meeting is one of the most significant features of the Congregational and Baptist traditions. The local congregation "directs its own affairs," subject to the leadership of the Spirit. "No outside body has authority over it except with its own consent. All members share equally in the decisions that are taken." [11] The business handled in such church meetings includes matters of government, membership, doctrine, the care of building and grounds, as well as discipline.

The church's discipline will always reflect the character of the church's doctrine. The latter in essence is unchanging because it grows out of the facts connected with God's self-revelation in history. The former by nature appertains to specific applications of this unchanging truth in constantly changing circumstances. It not only may change, it must change if it is to remain relevant. The opening paragraph of the preface to the *Book of Common Prayer* puts it in now classic form:

It is a most invaluable part of that blessed "liberty wherewith Christ hath made us free," that in his worship different forms and usages may without offence be allowed, provided the substance of the Faith be kept entire; and that, in every Church, what cannot be clearly determined to belong to Doctrine must be referred to Discipline; and therefore, by common consent and authority, may be altered, abridged, enlarged, amended, or otherwise disposed of, as may seem most convenient for the edification of the people, "according to the various exigency of times and occasions."

[11] E. A. Payne, *The Fellowship of Believers* (enlarged ed.; London: The Carey Kingsgate Press, 1952), p. 101.

Some indication of *the doctrinal temper* and bearing of the important early Baptist confessions—and especially their understanding of the nature of the church and of Christian fellowship—must, therefore, serve as preface to the statements on discipline in the stricter sense. Briefly to be considered are four early English confessions (two Particular and two General) and three American.

The London Confession of 1644 was prepared by the seven churches there. It is moderately Calvinistic and is said by McGlothlin [12] to be "the first Confession of history to prescribe a single immersion as the form of baptism." McGlothlin also felt (1910) this confession represented "the views of the Baptists of the world more nearly than any other . . ." [13] This confession is careful to disclaim the "Popish Doctrine" of church succession and is equally anxious to demonstrate that its subscribers are neither Anabaptists nor General Baptists.

Even more important, perhaps, was the Second London Confession of 1677, which, following the accession of William and Mary, was approved in London in 1689 by the assembly of representatives from 107 churches in England and Wales. This strongly Calvinistic confession rests directly on the Westminster Confession of 1648, as altered to suit Baptist understanding of the mode of baptism and nature of the church. In the address "To the Judicious and Impartial Reader," by which this confession is prefaced, the wish is affirmed to demonstrate "hearty agreement with . . . that wholesome protestant doctrine," which the Presbyterian divines had affirmed a generation earlier. Only on the "subject" of baptism is basic difference thought to obtain.

[12] W. J. McGlothlin, *Baptist Confessions of Faith* (Philadelphia: American Baptist Publication Society, 1911), p. 169.
[13] *Ibid.*, p. 170.

These two Calvinistic confessions may be balanced by two from the tradition of the General Baptists, who had been associated at the inception of their organized life in England with Thomas Helwys: the Standard Confession and the Orthodox Creed.

The Standard Confession of 1660 is one of the earliest General Baptist statements to prescribe dipping, or immersion, as the proper mode of baptism. This was probably a result, in part, of the influence of the Particular Baptist Confession of 1644. This group of Arminian Baptists were closer to the Dutch Mennonites in doctrine and in early practice of baptism than were the Particular Baptists. At the same time they announced that they were only falsely called Anabaptists.

The Orthodox Creed of 1678 is the next General Baptist confession of importance. In the Second London Confession of 1677 the Particular Baptists had revised the Westminster Confession and claimed large agreement with Presbyterians and Congregationalists. In the Orthodox Creed of 1678 the General Baptists sought "to unite and confirm all true protestants" in the fundamental articles of the faith against the errors of Rome.[14] This confession of 1678, put out by General Baptists, by its cautious approaches toward rapport with the system of Calvinistic Baptists marks an important anticipation of the work of Andrew Fuller and others in the latter part of the eighteenth century.

Of American confessions little need be said. The Philadelphia Confession of 1742, with additions of articles on "Psalm singing" and "laying on of hands," is an exact reprint of the Particular Baptists' Confession of 1677, as printed in 1689. Following the Philadelphia action, but omitting the laying on of hands, the Charleston Association adopted the same confession, 1767.

[14] Cf. *ibid.*, p. 123.

The New Hampshire Confession of 1833 is important for its being the first to drop from its articles the historic Baptist affirmation of belief in the "catholick" or universal church. It had in its preface (advertisement) a reference to "the Church" and to her "Great Head," but this preface is not commonly printed as a part of the confession. The preface is, for example, dropped from J. M. Pendleton's *Church Manual*, through which means it obtained a wide circulation in the South as well as North and West. Pendleton's use of the confession without preface helps one, in turn, to understand how the comparative "modernism" of the Landmark movement has successfully invaded the life of Southern Baptists. By the modernism of Landmarkism are meant especially two things that the Landmarkers introduced after 1850: (1) the unscriptural and non-Baptistic notion that the validity of church life and action depends on an institutional succession, called by whatever list of names, in history; and (2) the atomistic view of the church, denying the universal church which is Christ's body, in the name of the local church, a "voluntary association of baptized believers," nothing more. As every confession before 1833 testifies Baptist pioneers could believe in and magnify the local church precisely because it was the "outcropping" in its own community of the church universal. The historic Baptist position is that the local church has the fulness of churchmanship, both in dignity and in authority, just because in its own time and place it is the manifestation and embodiment of the wholeness of the church universal. The Scriptures teach the kingdom as the presupposition of church, and the church as the presupposition of the churches.

With this doctrinal introduction to the Baptist scene, and with these historic Baptist confessions serving as necessary context, the discussion of discipline proper may soundly be based on the London Confession of 1689, as reprinted in the Charleston (Charlestown) Confession and Summary of Discipline of 1774.[15]

The underlying motifs of this publication are: to witness to the truth in modesty and humility, to be perfectly candid with brethren of other names, to remove rather than to create a possible ground of contention, and to provide for adequate instruction in the faith in Christian homes.

The temper of the Charleston Confession, identical in principle with all Baptist confessions before 1833, is in vivid contrast to the distinctive affirmation of Landmarkism, noted above. It declares that "the Catholic or universal Church . . . consists of the whole number of the elect" and that this, the only true church, is "under Christ, the head thereof . . ."[16] As Head of the church, Christ is given "all power for the calling, institution, order or government of the church . . ."[17] Because all Christians are one in Christ, it is "for the good and prosperity of all the churches of Christ, in all places, and upon all occasions . . . to hold communion among themselves for their peace, increase of love and mutual edification."[18]

The section on discipline in the Charleston publication expresses the desire that its discipline as well as its doctrine be grounded on the Word of God. Its first four chapters are devoted to the church, church officers, reception into membership, and duties of members. But even after critical

[15] *A Confession of Faith, Put Forth by the Elders and Brethren of Many Congregations of Christians (Baptised upon Profession of Their Faith), in London and the Country,* Fourth Charleston Edition. (From a printing by E. Temple at Raleigh, N. C., 1850, that also contains *A Summary of Church Discipline; Showing the Qualifications and Duties of the Officers and Members of a Gospel Church,* by the Baptist Association in Charleston, S. C. and *The Baptist Catechism or, a Brief Instruction in the Principles of the Christian Religion Agreeably to the Confession of Faith.*)

[16] *Ibid.,* p. 53.
[17] *Ibid.,* p. 54.
[18] *Ibid.,* p. 57.

examination by the church and after showing adequate instruction in the faith, some Christians, because of sin and error, require censure by the church. This is the subject of chapter five of the Summary of Church Discipline.

According to chapter 5, Christ deals directly in some instances in dispensing reward and punishment. But "there are other punishments which Christ, by his word, authorized his church to inflict on its rebellious and unworthy members: These are commonly called church censures which differ in their nature according to the nature and degree of the offense; and may be denominated rebuke, suspension and excommunication." [19] These three may be examined as to their nature, occasion, and enforcement.

§ 1. Rebuke or admonition (the lowest degree of church-censure) is a reproving [of] an offender, pointing out the offence, charging it upon the conscience[,] advising and exhorting him to repentance, watchfulness and new obedience; and praying for him that he may be reclaimed . . . administered in love and tenderness . . . with Christian prudence . . . a sincere aim to save the soul from death . . . without partiality . . . and for a caution to others . . .

A member becomes worthy of rebuke, (1) When he wounds the conscience of a weak brother, by the use of things in themselves indifferent . . . (2) When he exposes the infirmatives [sic] of a brother to others . . . (3) When he disquieteth the peace of the brethren about matters of indifference . . . (4) When he indulges anger against a brother, without a just cause . . . (5) When he is contentious about unscriptural forms and fashions, as if they were necessary to be used in the church, or among the members . . . (6) When he neglects privately to admonish or reprove a brother whom he knows to be guilty of sin . . . (7) When he neglects to attend church-meetings for business . . . (8) When he attends other places of worship to the neglect of his own . . .[20]

[19] Page 19 in the printing cited above in footnote 15.
[20] Ibid., pp. 19–20.

The Charleston publication has little to say directly as to the manner of implementing this disciplinary procedure. On that side, the Philadelphia Discipline has this to offer:

Every church member has somewhat to do in his place . . . that private conference must precede any public action . . . that when the matter has been laid before the Church, all private proceedings must cease . . . that the Church as such is to deal with no case which has not begun in a private effort of reconciliation and reclamation.[21]

The Charleston Discipline goes on to say:

§ 2. Suspension, considered as a church-censure, is that act of a church whereby an offending member, being found guilty, is set aside from office, from the Lord's table, and from the liberty of judging or voting in any case . . . this censure doth not cut off from union, but only from communion with the church, [therefore] the suspended member is not to be accounted an enemy, but admonished as a brother . . . and upon credible profession of repentance, the censure is to be taken off, and the delinquent restored to all the privileges of the church.[22]

Those practices which in nature or tendency are destructive of the reputation, peace, and prosperity of the church but which do not appear to be past remedy come in this category. Suspension is administered for cases less grave than those requiring excommunication, as:

(1) When a member breaks the peace of the church by janglings and disputings . . . (2) When he withdraws from the church

[21] *A Confession of Faith, Put Forth by the Elders and Brethren of Many Congregations of Christians . . . in London and in the Country. Adopted by the Baptist Association, Met at Philadelphia, September 25, 1742.* Philadelphia: Printed and published by Anderson and Meehan, No. 59 Locust Street, 1818. The Philadelphia *Abstract of Discipline* is appended to the Confession.

[22] Charleston Discipline, pp. 20–21.

on account of its wholesome discipline, notwithstanding loving admonitions have been given him . . . (3) When he leaves his place at the Lord's table, for the sake of another member, with whom he is offended, and neglects to do his duty by him as directed . . . (4) When he broaches unsound heretical principles . . . (5) When he is a busy tatler, and backbiter . . . (6) When he, through sloth, neglects the necessary duties of life . . . (7) When he has committed a gross crime, but gives some tokens of repentance, he is to be suspended, that the church may have time to judge of his sincerity . . . (8) When a party of members . . . break through their covenant obligations, and attempt to set up for themselves, in an irregular manner, in opposition to all the loving persuasions of the majority; such are truce breakers, and despisers of those that are good . . .[23]

The Philadelphia Discipline adds nothing to this in principle. It does specify that where a suspended offender "remains impenitent and incorrigible, the Church, after due waiting for his reformation, is to proceed to excommunication."

The seriousness of excommunication is emphasized in the Charleston Discipline:

§ 3. As excommunication is, on all hands, acknowledged to be an ordinance of Christ . . . and a censure in its own nature, very important, awful and tremendous, it is highly needful that churches should well understand the nature of it.

Excommunication is a censure of the highest degree; it is a judicial act of the church, in which, by the authority of Christ, she cuts off and entirely excludes an unworthy member, from union and communion with the church; and from all the rights and privileges thereof. "It is a disfranchising from all the immunities of a fellow-citizen with the saints, and taking from him a place and a name in the house of God." [24]

It is stressed that this censure affects only the spiritual concerns of men and must involve no temporal or civil penalties,

[23] *Ibid.*, p. 21.
[24] *Ibid.*, pp. 21–22.

whether fines, imprisonment, death, or domestic disruption. Neither is attendance forbidden on the external ministry of the word.

The subjects of the ordinance of excommunication are those members "who are guilty of notorious and atrocious crimes . . ." The following offences "call for a speedy excommunication, unless the most evident marks of repentance appear in the offender, as (1) All sins that are against the letter of the ten commandments . . . (2) All that call for severe corporal punishment from human laws; provided those laws are not contrary to the laws of God . . . (3) All such sins as are highly scandalous in their nature, and expose the church to contempt." [25]

Both reason and the example of Christ, however, dictate forgiveness to the genuinely repentant. No member may excommunicate himself. He leaves the church only by the will of the church—just as he may enter it in the first place. A person guilty of leaving the church is a trucebreaker and ought to be avoided by other churches.

. . . This great censure is to be executed "by the elders [ministers] of churches, with the consent of the members of them; for they have a right to do this, previous to their having elders, and when they have none, as to receive members, so to expel them. The power of it originally lies in the church; the authority of executing it lies in the elders, with the consent and by the order of the church . . ." [26]

The solemnity of such a situation, as well as numerous implications as to the nature of the church as a disciplined community of believers, is evident in the following statement of proceedings:

[25] *Ibid.*, p. 23.
[26] *Ibid.*, p. 24.

To proceed regularly in this solemn business the church must cite such an accused member to appear, either at a stated church meeting of business, or at an occasional meeting for that purpose; in order that he may have a fair trial, and an opportunity of making his defence if he has any to make. The meeting is opened by prayer for direction; then the case is impartially examined into, and tried by the word of God; if the accused member is found guilty of a crime deserving excommunication, he is not to be immediately cut off (unless it be some extraordinary case) but admonished, and sometime given him for repentance and for the church to mourn over him and pray for him. If the offender continues obstinate, and appears to be incorrigible, the church is under a necessity of proceeding to the execution of the great censure against him.[27]

If the offense in case be of a private nature, then excommunication must be pronounced only before the church meeting; if it involves public scandal, then in public meeting conducted by the church. The service in which the sentence is passed consists of prayer for the offender, a sermon which dwells on the nature of the crime, the scandal brought on religion, and the load of sin and guilt. The excommunication aims, as a last resort, at the recovery of the offender and at warning others. Then, by the authority of Christ, in the name and behalf of the church, the offender is solemnly sentenced by name, being cut off from union and communion with the church.

The ends to be answered by this solemn ordinance, always to be held in view are: (1) the glory of God; (2) the purgation and preservation of the church; (3) the eradication of sin and error; and (4) the good of the person excommunicated.[28]

The Philadelphia Discipline is more explicit in matters of

[27] *Ibid.*, pp. 24–25.
[28] *Ibid.*, p. 26.

manners and order, as well as of heresy. For example, ex-communication is prescribed not only for heretics but also for such members as might divulge to persons not of the congregation what is done in the church meeting (p. 103 f.).

Summary and Application

One needs here to note a perennial contradiction which appears in the existence of the historic church. By faith the church is the divine community. By sin the church is the con-tradiction of her own gospel. As a congregation of saints the church knows God's demand. As being "at the time right-eous and sinful" the church must bring that demand to bear on sin and error. The church thus ever requires to be re-formed by the very truth she holds in trust. Certainly a claim to infallibility of teaching and irreformability of institutions is an indication more of pride than of grace and rests on no promise of the living Lord.[29] One thing, however, the church can do: She can be committed to the truth she already knows and faithful to the tasks she receives from her Lord. "By the rule whereunto she has already attained, by that same rule she can and must order her life." And another thing she can do: As sin and error arise in her midst, the church can correct these in love through mutual instruction, mutual re-buke, and mutual aid.

For a proper exercise of discipline in the church there must be a balance of freedom and responsibility. Ecclesiastical freedom which is uncontrolled by defined responsibility is anarchy. Responsibility defined in any manner which leaves

[29] All of Luther's Theses are relevant here, but surely the first is enough: "The whole Christian life is a life of repentance." Zwingli, in the *Com-mentary on True and False Religion*, even pointed out that the sure way the Christian knows that he is *alive* unto God is that he is in *active struggle* against sin and the devil.

the congregation no freedom to act is tyranny. Between the poles of individualistic anarchy and hierarchical tyranny the true *ecclēsia* is set. To belong to the church means both to have been committed to the highest personal responsibility and to have renounced all isolated individual existence. He only is free who, through the Son by the Spirit, is made utterly dependent upon the Father and who, through a common grace and calling, is entirely bound up with his fellows in the life of the body of Christ. The life of the church, then, is neither an individualism nor a collectivism. It is personal life under God, and with one another in God, on terms where no one's freedom outruns his obligation and every man's obligation is discharged in freedom.[30]

The relevance of the following remarks, it is hoped, will be obvious.

First, when respectability takes precedence of righteousness in the church of God, then the churches are too ashamedly self-conscious to maintain discipline. The prevalent sense of politeness would be gravely shocked at a church meeting where a fellow member's heresy is tried or his moral lapse investigated before the congregation. Christians thus have stopped mourning and praying over an erring brother that he might be reclaimed from the devil to the life of the church.

Second, the very essence of the New Testament *ecclēsia* —and one might add, of the early English and American Baptist churches—was personal fellowship in faith and service. People were not casually admitted to membership. Instruction in the biblical faith was required, and a more than merely emotional experience of grace had to be in evidence. Two implications appear from this situation: (1) that type of individualism which sees every man's religion to be his

---

[30] Cf. Emil Brunner, *The Misunderstanding of the Church* (London: Lutterworth Press, 1952), pp. 114 f.

own private business is a parody of the New Testament church; and (2) it is difficult for large congregations to be New Testament fellowships.

Third, Christian discipline, like Christian morality generally, can never properly consist in the mechanical application of a set of rules. The church herself stands under the judgment and grace of Christ, her living Head. She stands on the word of God, as the living intention of God voiced in revelation and redemption by his own Spirit. To this word, the Bible bears inspired and authoritative witness. Be it said for all the historic Baptist confessions and disciplines, they were meant to serve as helps and guides in understanding and applying the truth of Holy Scripture, and almost always they show sound Christian judgment on the manner in which permanent truth is to be applied in relative situations.

Finally, there is a current need to recover the sense of the dignity and authority of the church.[31] This is increasingly difficult for Southern Baptists to achieve within the greatly changed patterns of Southern life. In principle Baptists have viewed a church as a congregation of saints, have stressed informed and responsible discipleship on the basis of personal regeneration. The Christian life has been viewed as one of "separation from the world and unto God." But success itself has risen up to threaten this! In becoming a mass movement and, in the South, all but a territorial church, Baptists have found it difficult to be "separate." The Southern Baptist Convention is no longer in actual practice a group of "gathered and disciplined churches." The more Southern Baptists succeed—at the surface level of mere numerical increase without corresponding growth in biblical knowledge, theological competence, and ethical sensitivity—the more diffi-

[31] Cf. Eph. 4:12; 1 Tim. 3:15.

cult it will become for them to be as Baptist in fact as they are in name.

It is to this situation that a proper discipline must be directed. And it is, moreover, to this that realistic attention and earnest prayer need to be given.

ABOUT THE WRITERS

William Owen Carver was born in Wilson County, Tennessee, on April 10, 1868, and died in Louisville, Kentucky, on May 24, 1954. He became a member of the faculty of Southern Baptist Theological Seminary in 1895 and at the time of his death was professor emeritus of comparative religion and missions. He was a graduate of Richmond College (M.A.) and Southern Baptist Theological Seminary (Th.M. and Th.D.); he also studied at Oxford, England, and Berlin, Germany. Dr. Carver served as pastor of churches in Virginia, Kentucky, and Tennessee, as editor of the *Review and Expositor*, and as president of the Southern Baptist Historical Society. The author of 18 books, he also contributed to encyclopedias, journals, and magazines.

Robert W. Kicklighter, pastor of the Blackwell Memorial Baptist Church of Elizabeth City, North Carolina, since 1949, was born in Georgia. He earned the A.B. degree from John B. Stetson University and the Th.M. and Th.D. degrees from Southern Baptist Theological Seminary. During World War II Dr. Kicklighter served as a Navy chaplain; he has held pastorates in Florida, Indiana, and Kentucky. He is now a member of the Board of Trustees of Southern Baptist Theological Seminary and of the General Board of the Baptist State Convention of North Carolina and its Executive Committee.

Duke K. McCall is president of Southern Baptist Theological Seminary, Louisville, Kentucky. A native of Mississippi, he was educated at Furman University (A.B.) and Southern Baptist Theological Seminary (Th.M. and Ph.D.). Dr. McCall was

186

formerly president of the New Orleans Baptist Theological Seminary and, later, executive secretary of the Southern Baptist Convention's Executive Committee. He is now a member of the Baptist World Alliance Executive Committee, the board of visitors of the United States Air University, vice-president of the American Association of Theological Schools, and president of the National Temperance League. A frequent contributor to denominational publications, Dr. McCall is the author of *God's Hurry* and co-author of *Passport to the World* and *Broadman Comments, 1958.*

Dale Moody is Joseph Emerson Brown professor of systematic theology at Southern Baptist Theological Seminary, Louisville, Kentucky. Born in Texas, he attended Baylor University (B.A.), Dallas Theological Seminary, and Southern Baptist Theological Seminary (Th.M. and Th.D.). Elected fellow of the National Council of Religion in Higher Education, Dr. Moody received the Council's Kent Fellowship for study at Columbia University. He was later a student at the University of Zürich and the University of Basel. Dr. Moody has served as pastor of churches in Texas, Indiana, and Kentucky.

S. A. Newman, professor of theology and philosophy of religion at Southeastern Baptist Theological Seminary, Wake Forest, North Carolina, is a native of Texas. His educational background includes Hardin-Simmons University (A.B.) and Southwestern Baptist Theological Seminary (Th.M. and Th.D.). For a number of years Dr. Newman served as a member of the faculty in the philosophy of religion department and as registrar at Southwestern Baptist Theological Seminary. He was pastor of his home church in Jermyn, Texas, for 13 years. Dr. Newman joined the faculty of Southeastern in 1952.

Theron D. Price, who is David T. Porter professor of church history at Southern Baptist Theological Seminary, Louisville, is a native of Arkansas. He received degrees from Ouachita College (B.A.), Southern Baptist Theological Seminary (Th.M. and Th.D.), and Yale University (M.A.). Dr. Price has served as pastor of churches in Arkansas, Kentucky, and Connecticut; he is a member of the American Society of Church History and the American Society for Reformation Research. For three years he was professor of the history of Christianity at Mercer University, Macon, Georgia, and for one year, visiting professor of church history, Baptist Theological Seminary, Rüschlikon-Zürich, Switzerland.

T. C. Smith, associate professor of New Testament, Southern Baptist Theological Seminary, Louisville, Kentucky, is a native of Louisiana. His educational background includes study at Louisiana College (A.B.); Southern Baptist Theological Seminary (Th.M. and Th.D.); Edinburgh University, Edinburgh, Scotland (Ph.D.); Union Theological Seminary, New York; Regent's Park College, Oxford University, England; and Hebrew Union College, Cincinnati, Ohio. He has served as pastor of churches in Virginia, and Kentucky, as a Navy chaplain in World War II, and as review editor of the *Review and Expositor.* Dr. Smith now holds membership in the Society of Biblical Literature and Exegesis and *Studiorum Novi Testamenti Societas.*

Paul L. Stagg, pastor of the First Baptist Church of Front Royal, Virginia, since 1947, was born in Louisiana into a family active in pioneer missionary work among the French-speaking people there. He attended Louisiana College (B.A.) and Southern Baptist Theological Seminary (Th.M.) and studied at Columbia University and Union Theological Seminary. Mr. Stagg was an Army chaplain during World War II; he has held pastorates in Louisiana and West Virginia. He is a contributor to various magazines, Sunday school lesson writer for the American Baptist Publication Society, and a member of the Virginia (Baptist) Christian Life Commission and of the Board of Trustees of the *Religious Herald.*

John E. Steely is assistant professor of historical theology at Southeastern Baptist Theological Seminary, Wake Forest, North Carolina. A native of Arkansas, he received the A.B. degree from Ouachita College and the B.D., Th.M., and Th.D. degrees from Southern Baptist Theological Seminary. Dr. Steely has held several pastorates in Arkansas and Illinois; for several years he served as head of the Bible department of Southern Baptist College, Walnut Ridge, Arkansas. He later became dean of administration of that institution. Dr. Steely came to Southeastern Baptist Theological Seminary in the fall of 1956.

Robert G. Torbet is director of the Department of Educational Services of the Board of Education and Publication of the American Baptist Convention. He is a graduate of Eastern Baptist Theological Seminary in Philadelphia, where he later served for several years as professor of church history. He holds the Ph.D. degree from the University of Pennsylvania. From 1951 to 1955 he was editor of American Baptist Uniform Lessons and associate editor of the *Baptist Leader*. Dr. Torbet is the author of several books: *A History of the Baptists; The Baptist Ministry, Then and Now; Venture of Faith;* and *The Baptist Story*.